More Tales from the Red Sox Dugout

Yarns from the Sox

By
Jim Prime
and Bill Nowlin

Sports Publishing, LLC
www.sportspublishingllc.com

Director of production: Susan M. Moyer
Dust jacket design: Kenneth J. Higgerson

ISBN: 1-58261-635-3

Printed in the United States of America

Sports Publishing, LLC
www.sportspublishingllc.com

Front cover photo by Bill Belknap, *Boston Herald*
Back cover photo courtesy of AP/Wide World Photos.
*"Having A Field Day"—The front cover photograph depicts Ted
Williams atop a "midget auto" and was taken on August 22,
1958, at Fenway Park. The Northeast Shriners were in town for
a convention and a large number of them attended the ballgame.
Tris Speaker was honored in pre-game ceremonies and presented
with a "beautiful fez and plaque." The massed Canadian and
American Shrine bands played the national anthems of the two
countries. The Sox won 4-3. ted was 1-for-3, a single.*

To Glenna, Catherine, Jeffrey, Margaret,
Ray, Andrew, and Matthew.
And to the unsung heroes in all our lives.
—JP

To Yleana and to Emmet,
and this time to Johnny Pesky.
—BN

Acknowledgments

During the course of research for this book, we thank the following for interviews or information supplied: Joanne Alfieri, Paul Armstrong, Peter Bjarkman, Ben Robicheau, John Boggs, Todd Bolton (SABR Negro Leagues Committee), Greg Bond (Boston Red Sox), Debbie Matson (Boston Red Sox), Ken Coleman, Billy Consolo, Maureen Cronin, Paolo Dellasandro, Dom DiMaggio, Bobby Doerr, Walt Dropo, Nomar Garciaparra, Dick Gernert, Don Gile, Paul Gleason, Tim Horgan, Mike Ipavec, Jim Kaklamanos, Wendell Kim, Martin Kohout, Roger LaFrancois, Bill Lee, Don Lee, Ted Lepcio, John Lickert, Jim Lonborg, Ed Luteran, Shelley MacDonald, Frank Malzone, Marty Marion, Steve Mastroyin, Mickey McDermott, John Merian (El Tiante Cigars), Lou Merloni, Joe Morgan, Derek O'Grady, Cliff Otto, Mel Parnell, Eddie Pellagrini, Johnny Pesky, Dick Radatz, C. Paul Rogers III, Mary Jane Ryan (Boston Red Sox), Tim Samway, Tim Savage, Aaron Schmidt (Boston Public Library Prints Department), Jessica Smith (Boston Red Sox), Lyle Spatz, Greg Spira, Birdie Tebbetts, Dick Thompson, Luis Tiant, Luis Tiant, Jr., Edward Valentine, and Ted Williams. Special thanks to Dick Bresciani of the Boston Red Sox.

Contents

vi

Introduction

Just when you think you've heard them all, the Red Sox yarns keep unraveling. Some were buried deep in the dresser drawer like that proverbial odd sock, the one you save in hopes that its mate will someday turn up. *Tales From the Red Sox Dugout* presented some of the classic stories about the Boston Red Sox and their colorful, eccentric history. It also featured instant classics by and about current players such as Nomar Garciaparra and Pedro Martinez. The book hit a chord with Red Sox fans and baseball fans generally. In fact it proved to be such a success that Sports Publishing requested a sequel. *More Tales From the Red Sox: Yarns From the Sox* is the result. *More Tales* picks up the thread where the original left off. Writing about the Red Sox is like knitting a scarf for a giraffe: you could go on forever and never complete the job.

No, these stories are not just left over material from the original book. Every year you can count on the Bosox to come up with incidents and players who defy the imagination; every year another character knits another yarn or two. And every year you can count on guys like Mickey McDermott or Bill Lee to add some new patches to the Red Sox crazy quilt. In addition, readers of the original *Tales* approached the authors with other Red Sox stories—wonderful tales that we had missed first time around.

This book also offers some new twists. For one thing, Bill Nowlin's deeper involvement as co-author of *More Tales* adds a new dimension. Bill is steeped in Red Sox lore and has literally experienced Fenway Park from every possible angle—including from a perch inside the Green Monster's scoreboard. Bill is one of the few people to pull an all-nighter at the venerable old ballpark in order to observe it devoid of the presence of the madding crowds.

More Tales also includes a few jokes, and other features guaranteed to amuse, instruct and fascinate! There is even a non-human entry and one fictional pitcher of some fame.

Like most of you, we are both Red Sox fans. We know Ted Williams' birth date and we know how to spell Yastrzemski without checking them out in *Total Baseball*. Instead of counting sheep we often count the number of bounces the ball took before it went through Bill Buckner's legs, and we have Bucky Dent's likeness etched on the dartboards of our souls. We think that Bill Lee and Mickey McDermott are the baseball equivalents of Laurel and Hardy and that Rice and Lynn were a gift from a just God. We think that Jeter is a poor man's Nomar, that Pedro is the second coming of Cy Young, and that Rocket Roger is a schoolyard bully. We would rather see the Red Sox win the World Series than a quick end to the recession. In short, we are committed (and probably should be) Red Sox fans.

Yes, the Red Sox yarns keep unraveling. Some are intended to keep you in stitches, others to keep you warm on those nights when it is too cold to play baseball. We hope that the quality and quantity of our yarns will make you darn glad to part of a tight-knit group known as Red Sox fans.

Dale Alexander

Alexander is a forgotten Red Sox player, but in 1932, despite totaling only 392 at-bats, he led the league with a .372 average. Author Ed Walton documented how the Tennessee farmer's career came to an unexpected halt. Doc Woods, a former trainer for the Yankees, was hired and decided that a leg injury Alexander had suffered should be treated by heat therapy. He placed Alexander under a heat lamp and went out to check on how the game was going. It must have been a good one, because he forgot to go back in to check on Alexander, who was out for a couple of weeks after being cooked to a "well-done" degree. Talk about your red-hot hitters!

Harry Agganis

Harry Agganis' promising career was cut short when he died at the age of 25 in 1955. The man known as the Golden Greek appeared in an official capacity at both Braves Field and Fenway Park on the same day in 1954. He began the day by hitting a game-winning homer for the Bosox and ended it by receiving his Boston University degree in ceremonies at Braves Field. The former pigskin star at B.U. was one of the few to go from horsehide to sheepskin all in one day in two major league ballparks in two different leagues. We are not sure if there is a record for this sort of thing, but if there is, we're sure Harry holds it.

Billy Consolo was Agganis' teammate with the Red Sox. He has fond memories of the former football All-American, who could have been a pro on the gridiron as well as the diamond. "Man, I tell you, if you're talking about a man's man, it was Harry Agganis. When I was rooming with him in '53, the Cleveland Browns called him up saying, 'Otto Graham has retired and you're our number-one draft choice. You don't want to play baseball.' I heard all those conversations, man. He could have been a professional football player, quarterback for the Cleveland Browns."

Larry Andersen

In Red Sox lore, he will forever be known as the player whom Lou Gorman obtained for Jeff Bagwell. Larry Andersen was in his 13th year of baseball at the time, an excellent reliever. Gorman acquired him at a crucial point in the 1990 pennant race, and Andersen threw 22 innings, with 25 strikeouts compared to just three walks. His ERA was 1.23. He was extremely effective in helping the Sox to win the division by just two games over the Blue Jays. Meanwhile, native son Bagwell, born in Boston, became a star with Houston the very next year—and after 11 years with the Astros sports a lifetime .303 average with 349 homers and 1,223 RBI. Gorman has long been ridiculed but when the trade was made, it reflected good baseball sense.

Andersen was, in Floyd Conner's choice words, "the Steven Wright of baseball. He pondered such matters as why slim chance and fat chance meant the same thing, and how do you know when invisible ink is dry?" The reliever was puzzled by something he saw most every day: "Why does everybody stand up and sing 'Take Me Out to the Ball Game' when they're already there?"

Elden Auker

Ted Williams once told Elden Auker, "You're about the only friend I have who doesn't want something from me. You've never even asked for my autograph." Auker replied, "You never ask me for my autograph so why should I ask for yours?"

Before John Valentin (1992-2001), the only Red Sox players to wear a number 13 jersey were Bob Fothergill (1933), Elder Auker (1939), Reid Nichols (1985) and Billy Joe Robidoux (1990.) After five seasons with the Red Sox, Nichols was traded the year he donned the number. 1990 proved to be Robidoux's last year in the majors.

Jim Bagby

Red Sox reliever Jim Bagby was once warming up in the bullpen while consuming a hotdog. Cronin called the kid in the bullpen and said, "Tell Bagby to get in here." Bagby hands the hotdog to the kid. "What am I going to do with the hotdog, it'll get cold?" the kid says. Bagby said, "Well, who am I going to pitch to?" The kid said "DiMaggio, Henrich and Keller." Bagby said "Hold the f—ing hotdog, I'll be right back!"

Jack Baker

Late in the 1977 season, Jack Baker stepped to the plate for the Red Sox, and his first major league hit was a home run into the screen at Fenway. Was this a new "Home Run" Baker in the making? Not quite. This Baker lacked the Ruthian recipe. In 22 other at-bats at the tail end of 1977 and in three more in 1978, he only managed two other hits. The career .115 hitter moved on to another career—perhaps as a butcher, or candlestick maker.

Matt Batts

Blessed with one of the most fitting—and Suessian— names in baseball history, Batts once incurred the wrath of legendary Boston manager Joe McCarthy. In August of 1948, the Red Sox were locked in a pennant race with the Cleveland Indians. Indians sparkplug Lou Boudreau stole home against Red Sox pitcher Mickey McDermott and catcher Batts. McCarthy stormed out of the Red Sox dugout to dispute the call at home plate and ended his tirade by kicking Batts in the posterior. Or as Dr. Suess might put it: Manager Mac attacks Matt Batts' slats.

Rod Beck

Rod Beck wishes no one—especially his dental hygienist—had noticed. But the TV cameras caught it all one summer night in an inter-league game with the Expos in Montreal during the 2001 season. Beck, celebrating after a key strikeout, accidentally spit out his gum. Not missing a beat, Beck bent down, picked it up, and popped it back in his mouth. "Now it looks even more like I'm the dirt bag everybody thinks I am," Beck said. "It landed on the turf, not on the mound," he insisted. "It fell on a clean spot." But he admitted that had it landed in the dirt he still would have chewed it. "That had never happened before," he explained. "I considered that my lucky gum."

Moe Berg

On one 1937 trip between Washington and Philadelphia, the Red Sox had four players fluent in four languages on the team. Mel Almada was born in Mexico, Fabian Gaffke was German, Gene Desautels was French and Dom Dallessandro was Italian. Moe Berg was able to talk with each reasonably fluently. Impressive, but would he have been able to communicate with Jimy Williams in Jimywocky?

Moe Berg was a Phi Beta Kappa Ivy Leaguer (Princeton), a Rhodes Scholar and an attorney. Apparently Berg could write in Japanese, too. Once he startled some visitors from Japan by autographing their ball in Japanese. When Joe Garagiola described catcher's equipment as "the tools of ignorance," he was obviously not talking about Moe.

In the *Big Book of Jewish Baseball,* the author claims that catcher and part-time spy (or is it the other way around?) Moe Berg actually met with Albert Einstein in 1945. Now that would be a conversation worth recording. Berg reportedly impressed Einstein with detailed knowledge of his recent writings on atomic warfare. And then it was Berg's turn to be impressed when Einstein described an article that Berg had penned on the subject of catching. Little wonder! The physics of splitting the atom are one thing, but the physics of the knuckleball remain beyond the realm of human knowledge. The two men had something else in common; neither could hit worth a darn.

Berg was a back-up catcher and rarely started a game. Instead, he spent long periods of time warming up pitchers in the Red Sox dugout. So when manager Joe Cronin once brought him in to catch the final innings of a game, Berg broke up the dugout by loudly inquiring of Cronin, "Joe, I can't remember. Do the batters still get three strikes in this league?"

Berg graduated *magna cum laude* from Columbia University Law School and pursued the study of philosophy at the Sorbonne in Paris but in some quarters that just doesn't measure up with being able to deliver a whack on the head, a tweak of the nose or a poke in the eye. When a publisher approached Berg with an offer to pen his autobiography, it looked like Berg's fascinating life story would finally be told. Unfortunately, the editor mistakenly believed he was negotiating with Moe Howard of the Three Stooges, and when it was discovered that Berg was only a major league ballplayer and international spy, the offer was promptly rescinded.

Clarence "Climax" Blethen

Some major league ballplayers exit the game having left a mark on posterity; still others depart with a mark on their own posterior. Red Sox pitcher Blethen was one of those players who left little mark on the game, but the game made a distinct mark on him. He was once bitten on the butt by his own teeth! He wore dentures and placed them in his back pocket when he played. Maybe he didn't trust his 1923 teammates enough to leave them in the clubhouse. One day, on a slide into second base, the teeth snapped shut on part of his anatomy.

Wade Boggs

Ted Williams redux? Well, not quite maybe, but not bad. On the final day of the 1985 season, Boggs admits he was counting numbers, shooting for 240 hits which would represent the highest total since 1930. With 11 games left, he still needed 19 hits.

The last day, he still needed three, and John McNamara asked him how many at-bats he wanted. "I'll go 3-for-3 and come out of the game," replied Boggs. First two times up, he got a double and then a single. Next at-bat, he made an out. McNamara informed Boggs that with that 2-for-3 he was in a dead tie with Rod Carew for the batting title, and asked if Wade wanted to share the title or go for hit #240, possibly risking the loss of both goals. Boggs said, "Just give me another at-bat," and got his hit.

Boggs started the season going 3-for-4 and closed it the same way. On the season, he hit 187 singles, seven more than the previous A.L. record. He hit safely in 135 games, tying the major league mark set in 1930.

Boggs averaged .338 during his 11 years as a Red Sox, getting over 200 hits in seven straight seasons. Too often in the press for one escapade or another, Boggs "left the Red Sox for the Yankees becoming perhaps the only sports star ever to move to the Big Apple in search of anonymity."— Friend & Zminda

"According to *The Sporting News*, over the last four years, Wade Boggs hit .800 with women in scoring position." — David Letterman

Oil Can Boyd

Oil Can Boyd courted controversy during his fiery tenure with the Red Sox. General Manager Lou Gorman describes why, after the disastrous sixth-game loss to the Mets, Oil Can didn't pitch in Game 7 of the 1986 World Series.

"Then it all fell apart. The wild pitch. The error. Then the loss. We were devastated. The next day, we were rained out and I met with [manager] John McNamara about what we were going to do in the seventh game. Oil Can Boyd was fresh, rested, and wanted to pitch the game. But Mac decided to go with Bruce Hurst. Hurst had won two games already in that series, though he was going to go without his normal rest. If he got in trouble early, we were going to bring in Boyd, and then finish up with [Calvin] Schiraldi. We had the lead going into the sixth inning, but then Bruce started to get into trouble. We were going to go to Boyd, but we couldn't find him." Will McDonough, *(Boston Globe 4/8/2000)*

The Can recalled meeting The Kid: "The first thing Ted Williams ever said to me, he saw me throw in minor-league camp, the first time he ever seen me, he was standing behind the backstop, and I'll never forget the day, he called time and said, 'Holy Cow, if it ain't Satchel in reincarnation.' And from that point on, he has been so good to me, he used to say he wanted to represent me, he talked me into the big leagues. He pulled for me every day, with other coaches, he said 'I don't care who you're lookin' at down here, that's the man you should have your eye on.' He was always telling people who were in charge of things to keep their eye on me, and sayin' 'I want to represent him, I want to be his agent!'"

In Bruce Shalin's book *Oddballs*, Oil Can compares himself to Satchel Paige: "Satchel had to pitch five innings every day. He warmed up over a matchbox. I know those kinds of things were true because I came up with the same kind of makeup as a ballplayer, knowing that the things that they said may seem kind of farfetched, but they were true. I warmed up as a Little Leaguer, I used to be able to throw a curveball and drop it into a bucket on home plate. That's how I learned to make my curveball go down. I had a perfect curveball."

Bill Buckner

He won the National League batting championship in 1980 with a .324 average. He accumulated 2,715 career

Bill Buckner (Brace Photography)

base hits. He led the National League in doubles not once but twice. He drove in 110 runs for the Red Sox in 1985 and another 102 runs in '86. He was a team leader for the Red Sox, perhaps the most respected man on the team. Nevertheless, the man known as Billy Bucks is best remembered for a ball that eluded his grasp and led to the most disappointing loss in Red Sox franchise history. The ball that went through his legs untouched in Game Six is now the object of a rather dark sort of fame. It was purchased at auction by actor Charlie Sheen and now presumably is a conversation piece in some Beverly Hills home. The price of the infamous spheroid: $93,000 and a million broken New England hearts.

Buckner excelled in bases-loaded situations. With the bases full in the 1985 season, Buckner batted .389 (7-18). He did not strike out a single time, hit into no double-plays and drove in 21 runs.

Buckner's infamous misplay of the grounder in the '86 World Series has inspired jokes such as;

Q: "What do Michael Jackson and Bill Buckner have in common?"

A: "They both wear one glove for no apparent reason."

Buckner actually had an excellent lifetime .992 fielding average.

Rick Burleson

According to teammate Bill Lee, Rick Burleson, known to Red Sox teammates and fans as "Rooster", "was mad all the time. " During a 1977 game against the hated Yankees, Burleson even managed to take his anger out on an inanimate object. When the Yankee scoreboard encouraged cheers for Reggie Jackson, Burleson turned and yelled epithets at the blinking lights.

In his May 4, 1974 debut, a nervous bantam Burleson committed three errors.

Bill Lee remembers Rick Burleson as a typical middle-infielder in temperament. "He reminded me of Billy Martin a lot. He was a hothead. We were in an elevator once in Minnesota and some drunk made a derogatory comment about him and Rooster started pounding on him. And finally I said, 'Leave him alone, let him fall down. ' He was tough. He was pugnacious like all those middle infielders. Eddie Stanky, Don Zimmer, Billy Martin, Leo Durocher. They're all the same. They're all pains in the ass."

Jose Canseco

While with the Red Sox, Jose Canseco expressed some rather interesting views on fuel economy: "The faster you drive, the less time you spend with your foot on the gas."

Bernie Carbo

During the 1975 Red Sox run for the pennant, Laurie Cabot—a witch from Salem—attempted to energize Bernie Carbo's slumping bat by putting a spell on it.

In the summer of '75, Carbo crashed into the bullpen at Fenway Park in a successful effort to prevent a home run by the Yankee batter. The jarring contact with the wall caused him to lose the plug of tobacco he had been chewing, and Carbo held up the game for a full ten minutes while he looked for his missing "chaw" on the dirt of the warning track. When he finally found it, he put it back in his mouth and the game continued.

Bill Lee, unofficial leader of the subversive group known as the Buffalo Heads, was a good friend of Carbo. "All of the Buffalo Heads, except Bernie Carbo, were pitchers," he recalls. "Jenkins, Willoughby, Wise, and myself—Bernie just wanted to be in there, he didn't want to be left behind. There are a million Buffalo Head stories in the naked jungle. A lot of mean tricks were played on Bernie. He was very intuitive, not well educated, flew by the seat of his pants. I considered him like a negative barometer. If anything was going to go wrong, he'd give me foresight into it."

Bill Carrigan/Joe Kerrigan

Bill "Rough" Carrigan really lived up to his nickname. Carrigan single-handedly put an end to Ty Cobb's infamous practice of sliding into home with sharpened spikes raised. He tagged The Georgia Peach hard in the face with the ball in his hand. Cobb was out, and also knocked out, and carried out of Fenway on a stretcher. Carrigan was a good receiver and actually caught three no-hitters for the Sox.

A few years later, Carrigan was manager when young Babe Ruth joined the Sox. In his first 3 1/2 years, the Red Sox won two championships. Ruth called him "the greatest manager I ever played for"—despite the fact that Rough had once slugged the slugger.

The only manager to win back-to-back World Series titles who is not in the Hall of Fame is Bill Carrigan. His Red Sox won the 1915 and 1916 championships.

The naming of Joe Kerrigan as Sox skipper in August 2001 restored a name steeped in Red Sox club history. During the 1913 season, on July 14, William F. "Rough" Carrigan assumed the managerial reins at Fenway, and ran the club for the 1914, 1915 and 1916 seasons—winning the World Series in both '15 and '16. Though just 33 at the time, his wife was pregnant, and he left the game to start a family in his home state of Maine. Years later, he was lured back by new owner Bob Quinn and managed the Sox for three less-than-stellar seasons 1927-9 (well, to be blunt, Boston finished dead last all three years.)

As it turns out, Joe Kerrigan's tenure was brief (17-26, .395 winning percentage working with a team decimated by injuries and discord.) That .395 was still better than any of the last three years of Carrigan's second coming. Kerrigan (maybe the best pitching coach the Red Sox ever had and the man Dennis Eckersley called Stats Masterson) was relieved of his duties during spring training 2002, only the fourth manager in major league history to lose his position during the preseason. Except for the bizarre 1907 Sox season, which saw four managers at the helm, Kerrigan's was the shortest tenure of any manager. In 1907, Chick Stahl committed suicide on March 27 (apparently more related to his playing the field than the team's play on the field), George Huff quit after eight games, and then first baseman Bob Unglaub managed for 29. Cy Young managed on an interim basis for six games. Finally, a true man of the flannel—Deacon McGuire—finished out the season. McGuire batted .750 that year in four well-chosen plate appearances.

Managers with even worse statistical records than Kerrigan's include Del Baker, Shano Collins, Lee Fohl, Marty

McManus, Heinie Wagner, and Rudy York—as well as Huff and Unglaub.

Roger Clemens

And he's thinking of wearing a New York cap into the Hall of Fame? During the 1986 World Series with the Mets, one of the problems the Red Sox players had to endure was the treatment they suffered from the security forces at Shea Stadium. Roger Clemens, in his book *Rocket Man*, recalls, "I have nothing against the fans, who except for a few nuts were fine. It was the security—the police and the way the place was handled. The security guards were screaming at our wives. . . . There was the fan who threw the golf ball out of the upper deck that just missed Rice's head. When we were coming in from the bullpen after we'd lost the final game, there were all sorts of security guards screaming obscenities at us and calling us all kinds of names." On the way to the bus, someone threw a can that hit traveling secretary Jack Rogers on the head and knocked him unconscious. As he lay there bleeding, Clemens says two New York cops stood around snickering.

When the Red Sox clinched the 1986 pennant, Texan Roger Clemens celebrated like a true cowboy. "One of the Boston policemen was on a horse named Timothy, and Rice yelled, 'There's your horse, Tex, get on it.' I looked up at the policeman, asked if I could get up there, and he said sure. When I got up and started riding around, the fans went crazy. . . . I can imagine what the Red Sox and the fans would have thought if I had fallen off. I've been riding all my life, so they shouldn't have worried, but since I was in back of the policeman and far back on Timothy, I put too much pressure on his bladder, he started bucking, and I did nearly get thrown off. I got off—in a hurry."

When Roger's first child Koby was born, Roger carried around a baseball card that indicated that Koby is a switch hitter and then the following: career highlights "In the year 2005, he stars at the University of Texas in baseball, beats Arizona State for the national title, and catches winning touchdown pass to beat Oklahoma 21-14 in Cotton Bowl."

Roger also says: "I'm the kind of guy who likes to eat cereal in the morning while I'm watching TV in my undershorts." Which inspired *Baseball Cards* columnist Irwin Cohen to quip: "To paraphrase Groucho Marx, how the TV got in his undershorts we'll never know."

In a memorable game in Oakland, Roger Clemens wore eyeblack and Ninja Turtle shoelaces and told umpire Terry Cooney, "I know where you live!" Just another one of those flaky northpaws that Bill Lee is always talking about.

Roger Clemens won his sixth Cy Young Award in 2001. Red Sox fans are still trying to figure out how a guy who was once a hero in Boston could manage to rack up seasons like his last four with the Red Sox:

1993   11-14   4.46 ERA
1994   9-7   2.85 ERA
1995   10-5   4.18 ERA
1996   10-13   3.63 ERA   total of 40-39

and then go on to win three Cy Youngs in the next five years.

Is Roger Clemens really the anti-Christ? It's been said that Clemens—this six-time Cy Young winner—doesn't really have any fans. He's burnt too many bridges in both Boston and Toronto, and never really earned a true fan base in New York. He may wear a Yankees cap into Cooperstown, but will anyone really care?

He began as a true hero in Boston, but (in Will McDonough's words) "put it on cruise control his last four years in Boston, allowing himself to balloon like the poster child for the Pillsbury Doughboy, letting his fastball drop to the high 80s, making sure he didn't get hurt." He said if he ever left the Red Sox, it would be to move closer to his home outside Dallas. He went to Toronto and immediately won two Cy Youngs there. He'd arranged and then invoked some clause in his contract—it was never fully explained—which resulted in the Blue Jays trading him to the Yankees.

There's one entire website devoted to anti-Roger material. Hating Roger has become an acceptable popular pastime in Boston. When the Yankees last visited Fenway in the 2001 season, sports talk radio station WEEI printed up thousands of cardboard posters as a giveaway promotion prior to the game. The posters read: WE HATE ROGER.

A few Clemens quotes of note from the website:

"I wish he were still playing. I'd probably crack his head open to show him how valuable I was." —Roger on Hank Aaron, after baseball's home run king suggested that pitchers should not be eligible for the MVP award.

"I thought it was the ball." —Roger, who apparently wanted to throw the baseball at Mike Piazza, on throwing a splintered bat at the Mets catcher.

"I could never come back and pitch against the Red Sox, so it would have to be in the other league." —Roger, as quoted by Will McDonough of the *Boston Globe*

"I've thrown the ball well in postseason play." —Roger, after being beaten by Pedro Martinez in the 1999 ALCS, comparing his 1-2 record in nine postseason starts with Boston versus Pedro's 3-0 career during the playoffs.

"I think undercover [Red Sox fans] are going to be rooting for me, too." —Roger, before being booed and taunted mercilessly by Red Sox nation at Fenway Park during Game 3 of the 1999 ALCS.

"I would only leave Boston to go back to Houston to be closer to my family." —Roger, as quoted by Will McDonough

"I have all the nice things in life because of the fact that [Red Sox owner] Mr. Harrington took care of me. I don't need a lot of money." —Roger, also as quoted by McDonough

"You just don't leave the Sox to go to the Yanks. That's like a black man joining the KKK," wrote an anonymous poster. "Roger Clemens represents everything that's wrong with sports today," editorialized the webmaster.

But is he really the anti-Christ? Bill Simmons of ESPN.COM said his bosses at ESPN gave him the following assignment: "Please explain to the world why Boston fans believe that Roger Clemens might be the anti-Christ." One suspects that Bill needed little prompting. "With pleasure, " he wrote and then launched into a 3,325-word diatribe.

Reggie Cleveland

Red Sox pitcher Reggie Cleveland rolled his car over in a Storrow Drive tunnel, reportedly while reaching into the back seat for a doughnut. That inspired this immortal line from Dennis Eckersley reported by Gordon Edes: "We need driver's ed, not a pitching coach."

Cleveland was one of the rare Red Sox to hail from Swift Current, Saskatchewan, Canada. "He dressed like Herb Tarlek from WKRP," says teammate Bill Lee. "He's probably a used car salesman somewhere. His weight used to fluctuate 15 pounds between starts."

Eddie Collins

While still a player, future Hall of Famer Eddie Collins —who went on to become Red Sox GM and was instrumental in signing a young prospect named Ted Williams— always placed his chewing gum on the button on top of his cap for good luck. It must have worked; Collins was one of the first major leaguers to accumulate over 3,000 career hits. Like many ballplayers of his day, Collins had other quirks. He used to bury his bats in shallow graves to keep them lively. In the midst of the 'dead ball era,' it kind of makes sense . . . no, wait a minute, we take that back. It makes no sense at all.

Tony Conigliaro

Before becoming the Red Sox manager and leading them to the 1967 "Impossible Dream " pennant, Dick Williams was Tony C's teammate. Management requested that he room with the handsome young star in order to provide some positive influence from a major league veteran. There was only one small flaw in the strategy. "Never saw him," claimed Williams in his book *No More Mr. Nice Guy.* "Not late at night, not first thing in the morning, never. I was providing veteran influence to a suitcase."

Like crooner Mickey McDermott before him, Tony C became a New England singing idol as well as a baseball

Tony Conigliaro (Brace Photography)

idol. It began with him singing old rock & roll songs with teammates Rico Petrocelli and Mike Ryan but quickly grew more serious as record companies tried to cash in on his huge popularity in the Boston area. His first big chartbuster was the aptly named "Playing the Field", with "Why Don't They Understand?" on the flip side. His Red Sox teammates went out of their way to keep the young heartthrob humble. When the record was first released Conigliaro rushed to the ballpark before the players arrived and left a copy in each of his teammates' lockers. He then went onto the field to work out. When he returned expecting congratulations and gratitude, he was greeted instead with stony silence. "What happened to the records?" he asked. One of the players motioned toward the trash barrel, overflowing with Tony C's records. Conigliaro immediately saw what was going on and laughed harder than anyone.

Marty Cordova

During the 2000 season, a short-staffed Boston newspaper was forced to send a non-baseball person to Fenway Park to interview former Red Sox player Marty Cordova. Cordova had been released by the Red Sox during spring training a few months earlier and this was his first time he'd visited Boston since his release.

On entering the visitors' dressing room, the apprehensive newsman approached the man he believed to be Cordova and tentatively began asking him questions. To his surprise and delight the ballplayer responded vigorously to his inquiries. He was obviously a man who wanted to vent his feelings to the public following a terrible injustice. Warming to his task, the reporter asked Cordova to expand on his feelings about being released—whereupon the ballplayer launched into a passionate, vitriolic diatribe on the entire Red Sox organization from top to bottom. He condemned the team and everyone associated with it, past and present. He concluded by stating that the Boston Red Sox were the most despised franchise in sport and that he would exact revenge upon them if it took him the rest of his natural life. The reporter was flushed with success. He thanked the ballplayer profusely for his frankness and headed for the door, thoughts of Pulitzers no doubt dancing in his head. Just as he was about to exit the room, the irate ballplayer hailed him once again. "I have one more thing I want to add," he said. "What's that?" asked the eager reporter, tape recorder poised to capture more venomous rhetoric. "I'm John Frascatore," he said. "That's Cordova over there."

Joe Cronin

"Curt Gowdy once told me that Yawkey fired my dad at least twice a week," says Joe Cronin's daughter Maureen. "Ten times more than Steinbrenner fired Billy Martin, because Yawkey was a big drinker and he'd have a few and say 'You're fired!' I mean it was kind of a joke, but I felt badly for my poor dad."

On August 25, 1937, the Red Sox faced Cleveland ace Bob Feller. Rapid Robert proceeded to strike out 16 Red

Joe Cronin (Brace Photography)

Sox hitters en route to a four-hit, 8-1 victory. After being called out on strikes for his second strikeout of the day, Red Sox player-manager Joe Cronin turned to umpire Lou Kolls and asked reasonably, "If I can't see it, how did you see it?"

When Cronin became General Manager of the Boston Red Sox, he soon had old friends from the west coast calling to ask favors. Frank Keneally, a fan of the San Francisco Seals and an old school friend of Cronin's, called to urge Cronin to send a few expendable Red Sox players west to help out his team. Faced with lineup problems of his own, Cronin had to refuse the request. A few weeks later Keneally was reading the San Francisco newspapers and noticed that the Red Sox were mired in the depths of the American League standings while the Seals were near the top of their league. He rushed to send a telegram to Cronin: "Dear Joe—maybe we can help you."

As a player Cronin was good enough to be named All-star shortstop seven times by *The Sporting News* and capture an American league MVP award in 1930; as a player-manager he led teams to two pennants. He then became general manager of the Red Sox before becoming president of the American League.

He was one of the most successful pinch hitters in major league history. On a record five different occasions in 1943, Cronin, at the ripe old baseball age of 37, called his own number to pinch hit and responded with a home run each time. In total, the player-manager went to the plate 49 times in the pinch-hitting role and produced seven bases-on-balls, nine singles, four doubles, and five homers. In short, the man who earned the nickname "Mr. Clutch" set the standard for pinch hitters of his or any era. Former sports editor Bob Broeg of the *St. Louis Post-Dispatch*, in his book *Superstars of Baseball* summed it up nicely:

"Cronin in a pinch was Capt. Blood, a swashbuckler. In the era of the playing managers, a period of considerable color, charm and drama, Joe would put himself on the spot with a flair and courage that would make lesser men gulp." For his part, Cronin was much more modest about his pinch-hitting accomplishments. "I pulled rank and waited until the wind blew out," he claimed.

Brawls between the Red Sox and Yankees are as predictable as Harry Potter sequels, and almost as entertaining. On May 30, 1938, the Red Sox were playing a doubleheader with the Yankees in front of a capacity crowd of 83,533 at Yankee Stadium in the Bronx. In the first game Red Sox pitcher Archie McKain threw a purpose pitch a bit too close to Yankees batter Jake Powell. Powell charged the mound with his mind on mayhem, but his progress was blocked by shortstop-manager Joe Cronin. As the benches emptied and fists flew, Cronin protected his pitcher from several wayward punches. "We couldn't afford to have our pitcher ejected for fighting," he explained later. Cronin and Powell were tossed from the game by umpire Cal Hubbard, and order was eventually restored. However, as the ejected manager headed for the showers he was physically assaulted by several Yankee players in the tunnel leading to the Red Sox locker room.

When umpire Hubbard glanced at the Yankees dugout and saw it was vacant he rushed to the scene and attempted a rescue. "Three or four of them were going to town on poor dad," recounts Cronin's daughter Maureen. "They were beating him up and Cal Hubbard appeared.

Cal was huge, he used to play against Bronko Nagurski, so he knew how to handle the rough stuff." Hubbard, it should be noted, is the only person to be inducted into the baseball, college football and pro football halls of fame. The former Green Bay Packer stood an imposing 6-foot-4 and tipped the scales at 255 pounds. "This big hand came down and grabbed dad by the collar and pulled him out of this melee. Years later, when dad was made president of the American League, he made Cal Hubbard his chief of umpires."

Bill Crowley

Bill Crowley first joined the Red Sox as one of Curt Gowdy's broadcast partners in 1958. He went on to become the longtime Director of Public Relations for the Boston ballclub. It was his job to let both reporters and the general public know about the latest developments within the franchise and thereby build interest in the Red Sox. In 1972, when superstar pitcher Vida Blue was in a contract dispute with Charlie Finley and the Oakland Athletics, it was rumored that Blue was about to be dealt to the Red Sox. A reporter finally asked Crowley if he'd heard the rumor about Blue coming to Boston. "Hear it?" replied Crowley with a twinkle in his eye. "I started it. "

Tom Daly

Red Sox coach Tom Daly twice resorted to extraordinary measures to bring players down a notch. Buck "Bobo" Newsom was always going on about his pitching so one day Daly, a former catcher, challenged him, "Come on, Bobo," he said. "I'll warm you up bare-handed." And he did. His hand hurt for weeks, but he effectively silenced Bobo. He probably wouldn't want to try that with Pedro or Roger.

Then there was Wes Ferrell, who'd often state, "I can lick any man in checkers." Daly bought some books and studied up on checkers, then took Ferrell up on the challenge and beat him six games straight. Ferrell threw the checkerboard out the window.

Brian Daubach

Brian Daubach had played minor league professional baseball for nine frustrating seasons before finally signing a Red Sox contract. Brian is only the third left-handed Red Sox rookie to slam over 20 home runs; Ted Williams and Fred Lynn were the others. Ten of his home runs either tied the score or put the Red Sox ahead. All told, he had 27 game-tying and go-ahead RBIs.

It is only fitting that Daubach is one of the famed "Dirt Dogs", blue-collar players with a down-and-dirty work ethic. His brother Brad worked on Fenway's ground crew during the 2001 season. They obviously have dirt in their blood.

If you can picture China's Chairman Mao sitting down with Microsoft's chairman Bill Gates, if you can picture the proverbial lion laying down with the proverbial lamb, then maybe you can see Brian Daubach and Tim Wakefield hanging out together. Wakefield is a strong union man and the Red Sox union representative. Daubach, in some players' minds, is a scab, a hated "replacement player" who undermined the Major League Players Association back in the great strike of '95 (This is ironic because Brian came from a blue-collar background; his father Dale is a letter carrier for the U. S. Postal Service. Little wonder he has been delivering for the Red Sox ever since.) Why then were Daubach and Wakefield seen fraternizing like old buddies at a recent sporting event (well, actually a wrestling event) at the Fleet Center?

Daubach was there with his good friend Trot Nixon, another Red Sox "dirt dog" and several other players, including Wakefield. As *Boston Herald* writer Steve Buckley put it so very well, "Understand that Wakefield, in addition to being a knuckleball pitcher, is also a knuckle-fisted union man. He is John L. Lewis, Samuel Gompers and Marvin Miller rolled into one, yet he appears to have enormous respect for Brian Daubach, player, as well as Brian Daubach, person."

For some reason, Daubach's career numbers against pitchers from Aruba (population: 62,000) now include at least five home runs. He has two lifetime dingers off Calvin Maduro and three off Sidney Ponson. Next challenge: those pesky pitchers from the Outer Hebrides.

Dom DiMaggio

Dom DiMaggio was a smaller, bespectacled version of his brother Joe. The "Little Professor" had more total hits than any other player during the years he played, 1940-52 (excluding war years) and only Williams and Musial had more doubles over that same stretch. Only Ted scored more runs than Dom in the same period. He averaged 104.6 runs scored per season over his career. He is the only player NOT in the Hall of Fame to have done so. In the HOF, only Lou Gehrig and Joe DiMaggio rank higher.

Player-manager Joe Cronin was very close to DiMaggio and was responsible for getting Joe's little brother to play for the Red Sox. "Dad was one of the first to convince him that he could play the game with glasses," recalls Maureen Cronin. "He was from San Francisco, played on the same sandlot that my dad had played on. Dad had known Dom through Joe. They grew up in the same neighborhood. That's why he was very quick to look at Dom." Dom himself said, "The greatest satisfaction I have in baseball is that I broke in wearing glasses, and in those days, an athlete wearing glasses was a no-no."

"Being the lead-off man, Dom had the toughest job in the lineup," said Mel Parnell. "If he made an out he had to come back to the dugout where Ted Williams would grill him about where the pitch was, what the ball was doing, and what the pitcher had. He got the third degree from Ted."

Bill Dineen

Bill Dineen threw a no-hitter for the 1905 Red Sox, then known as the Boston Pilgrims. After his 12-year major league career was over, he worked for another 29 years as an American League umpire. This transition from player to umpire is rare enough but Dineen is the only major leaguer to have both pitched and umpired a no-hitter. In fact, he umpired six no-hitters in his career.

Bobby Doerr

Bobby Doerr was a pitcher's worst nightmare. He broke up a no-hitter against Spud Chandler in front of 69,107 fans at Yankee Stadium on July 2, 1946. On two other occasions, Doerr had the only hit in games the Sox played against Bob Feller.

Doerr was the only Sox player to hit for the cycle twice — in 1944 and 1947. He also batted in over 100 runs in six consecutive seasons with the Red Sox. The Hall of Fame second baseman combined with Vern Stephens in 1948 to drive in 248 runs and in 1949, the dynamic duo knocked in another 268. In 1950, they plated 264 of their team-mates.

Midway through his 13th season in the majors, right after throwing his third no-hitter, Bob Feller was asked to name the four toughest hitters he'd ever faced. Three of them were Red Sox: Feller named Joe DiMaggio, Ted Williams, Johnny Pesky and Bobby Doerr.

Patsy Donovan

Unlike Johnny Cash's "Boy Named Sue," Sox manager Patsy Donovan made no effort to compensate for his less than manly name by acting extra macho. Donavan hated obscenity. "Tish, tish," he told players, or "Tut, tut, boys, please don't say those words."

Lib Dooley

Lib Dooley was arguably the most loyal fan in Boston Red Sox history. Although obviously it is impossible to measure such things, her friend Ted Williams, who knows something about greatness, called her "the greatest Red Sox fan there'll ever be" and that's good enough for us. Lib was known among Red Sox management, players and fans as

"The Queen of Fenway Park" and her distinctive broad-brimmed hats and bright, elegant clothing made her stand out in any company, let alone in a time-worn ballpark such as Fenway. Dooley saw more than 4,000 consecutive games at Fenway Park and was a close friend of many Red Sox players, past and present, including Johnny Pesky, Bobby Doerr, Williams, Dom DiMaggio and Nomar Garciaparra. She baked cookies for many of them over the years and continued to send Ted Williams—who she considered a brother—some of his favorite foods up to the year of her death.

She didn't forget the batboys or the home plate umpires at Fenway either. Lib always had a little tray ready on the wall that separated her front row seat from the field of play. On it, she placed little cookies and bite-size candy bars for the boys with the bats and the men in blue.

Dooley started attending games at Fenway Park during WW II and hadn't missed one until illness finally ended her consecutive game streak in 1999. It was a record for longevity that even Cal Ripken could envy.

Lib was modest about her father John S. Dooley's role in Boston baseball. He was one of the key organizers of one of the early booster clubs, the Winter League. At the turn of the century, when Ban Johnson was attempting to place an American League franchise in Boston, the team lacked a suitable playing field. Jack Dooley facilitated contact with the Boston Elevated Railway, which owned the old Huntington Avenue Grounds—then a dump—and helped bring both parties together. That field became the first home park of the team later renamed the Red Sox and served as site of the first World Series, played in 1903.

Mr. Dooley also played a role in having the ban on Sunday baseball in Boston lifted in the 1930s. Elizabeth Dooley came by her passion for the Red Sox as part of a family tradition. Her father, as a young boy, attended the first baseball game ever played under electric lights, in 1880.

Lib died at the age of 87—Fenway was just one year older than she—in June of 2000, just shy of 120 years after her father had been to that first night game in Nantasket. The baseball gods paid a strange tribute to her. The Red Sox went out that day and lost to the Yankees 22-1, the worst home loss in their history.

Patsy Dougherty

Ironically, it may have been a Boston writer who gave the arch-rival Yankees their nickname. The reference to "Yankees" was first noted in a *Boston Herald* article of June 21, 1904, regarding the trade of Patsy Dougherty to New York for Bob Unglaub.   DOUGHERTY IS A YANKEE was the headline. Since this time, Red Sox fans have coined a lot of less printable names for their A.L. foes.

Dougherty hit three triples in one game, September 5, 1903. He led the league in hits that year, then hit two home runs in Game Two of the first World Series. Dougherty, in 1904, led the league in runs (as he had in 1903) with 113— 33 for Boston and 80 for New York.

Walt Dropo

The only major league player to ever hit a baseball over the Great Wall of China was Walt Dropo. Quite a number of years after his playing days were over, Dropo was working for a fireworks company and had occasion to visit China on business. Dropo told us, "About six months before I visited China, Bob Hope went over there and he hit a golf ball with a 9-iron over the Great Wall. I just took it on myself to bring a bat and a ball from the United States. I had my little niece throw me a pitch and I hit it over the Great Wall of China. The Wall wasn't that high."   Was there anyone on the other side to catch it, hoping for a souvenir? "The Mongolians were over there."

Dropo was Rookie of the Year in 1950, but he first played in Fenway Park way back in 1943, and his manager was none other than Babe Ruth himself! The game was an exhibition contest to raise money for the war effort. Dropo was 20 years old at the time, drafted out of the University of Connecticut and serving in the army at Fort Devens. "I played for the base team," the Moose from Moosup remembers. "They sent down a couple of us to that game to represent Fort Devens." He played first base, but went 0 for 2 while teammate Ted Williams (Also playing for Ruth's squad) took left field, went 2 for 4 and homered, driving in four runs. Dom DiMaggio tripled and drove in two as Ruth's All-Stars beat the Boston Braves 9-8.

Dennis Eckersley

Dennis Eckersley had two stints with the Red Sox and became an instant fan favorite throughout New England. He was a 20-game winner his first year in Boston—1978— though he also led the league in home runs surrendered.

Would that another pitcher on the team had won just one more regular season game that year! His next year was equally strong, though the team was not.

In 1984, Eck and Mike Brumley were traded to the Cubs for Bill Buckner, but his greatest years were with the Oakland A's where he was *Sporting News* Fireman of the Year in 1988, 1991 and 1992. Eck also appears on that publication's list of baseball's 100 greatest players. In the 1988 playoffs, he actually saved every one of the four games the A's won. In 1992 he won the A.L. Cy Young and MVP awards. Eckersley holds the American League record for the most saves with 390. In addition he also boasts three All-Star Game saves.

Part of Eck's popularity was his style. With his trade-mark long flowing hair and mustache he looked more like Zorro about to skewer the bad guys than a major league pitcher. He was equal parts Errol Flynn and The Rock. His colorful language and enthusiastic mound demeanor only added to his heroic aura. He threw a no-hitter the year before he joined Boston, and as it came down to the final out of the game, The Eck recalled later, "I was ready, but Gil (Flores) kept on stepping out of the box. I pointed at him,

Dennis Eckersley

'Get in there. They're not here to take your picture. You're the last out. Get in there.' I was pretty cocky back then!"

However, arrogance in an athlete is only bad if he can't back it up and Eckersley could definitely walk the walk. He had tremendous control, and in 1989 walked only three batters! In 1990 he only walked four in a total of 114 innings of relief work!

Once when Eckersley was in the midst of throwing a no-hitter for Cleveland against the California Angels, he got two strikes on the batter and turned to the on-deck circle, pointed at Jerry Remy and yelled, "You're next!" Later, Eckersley and Remy became teammates on the Red Sox.

Late in 2001, Eckersley became the national spokesman for Fire Prevention Week for the National Fire Protection Association. This wasn't just because he had been named "Fireman of the Year" three times. It resulted from a family incident when Eckersley's five-year-old son Jake registered his first save.

"It was December and my wife Nancy was working on making a cozy fire in our fireplace. Without warning, the fire shot back at her, and suddenly her hair was engulfed in flames." Eck wasn't home, but their son had learned a lesson he'd been taught at school. "My boy instinctively yelled, 'Stop, drop and roll,' and thankfully Nancy found the ability to respond through the chaos," Dennis explained. Nancy's hair was burned, but she was otherwise OK.

"We know of Dennis' reputation for saving games," said Meri-K Appy, Vice President of Public Education for

NFPA. "Now we're excited that he is helping us to save lives."

The Eck was worshipped in Cleveland, Boston and Oakland, beloved for his style and flair, his performances and his colorful sayings. Converted to a reliever a few years after leaving Boston, he ranks third on the all-time save list with 390. As Friend and Zminda wrote, "But with the attention and adoration came problems. He partied too hard, drank too much. In 1986, Eckersley decided to go into rehab and came out dry. That he stayed that way is probably his greatest save."

Eck-cetera:

Eckersley was responsible for coining a number of unique baseball terms, including the expression "walk-off home run." The Eck was inspired to utter the words for the first time after giving up a homer to Kirk Gibson in Game Two of the 1988 World Series. The term comes from all the players exiting the field as the winning run scores.

Other unique words in the Eckersley vocabulary include "oil", which was his term for liquor, long before "Oil Can" Boyd arrived on the scene. Money was known to Eck as "iron." He called himself "the Bridge Master," and if he surrendered a home run he said that he'd been "taken to the bridge."

Howard Ehmke

You win some, you lose some, and some are snatched rudely from your grasp by the fickle finger of the official scorer. Howard Ehmke won a no-hitter in 1923 despite giving up a double. Slim Harris (the pitcher for the other team) hit a double but missed touching first on his way to second and was thus ruled out. It was the only hit (not!) of the game for Ehmke's opponents. His next time out, a week later, Ehmke probably pitched another no-hitter—that he didn't get credit for. The leadoff batter reached on a "scratch roller" off the third baseman's glove. The official scorer ruled it a hit, though many considered it an obvious error. Ehmke only allowed one other Yankee base runner, a walk. Thus was Ehmke denied the glory later accorded Johnny Vander Meer for his consecutive no-nos. The Red Sox got six hits and won the September 11 game, and Ehmke had three of the six.

Ehmke was a 20-game winner that year totaling almost a third of Boston's wins as the Red Sox finished last with a pitiful 61 victories.

Dwight Evans

Even Harry Potter isn't as superstitious as these major league muggles! When a game in Seattle went into extra innings, Red Sox players wore their caps backwards to inspire a rally. The hometown Mariners countered by wearing their chapeaus inside-out and backwards, bending the brims to make them more streamlined. Not to be outdone, some Red Sox taped batting gloves on the ends of bats and used them as fishing poles while other bench-warmers placed Dixie cups over their ears and lathered their faces in shaving cream.

When Dwight Evans homered in the top of the 14th inning and eventually won the game for the Red Sox, the efforts of the bench crew took prominence over Evans' on-field heroics.

Dewey was infected by some of the same disease that gripped certain other players in the cramped, combustible Boston clubhouse. Con Chapman reports a pecking order established amongst the players. Newcomers who came over to Boston from other clubs noticed that batting practice pitchers threw fresh, white baseballs to the regulars and the more scuffed ones to the benchwarmers. When new utilityman Jack Brohamer moved to the post-game spread a little too quickly, Evans brusquely yelled, "You can't eat the spread until the regulars have had it." And Mike Greenwell took umbrage to rookie Mo Vaughn's lining up for batting practice ahead of Greenwell. Some pushing resulted, and Greenwell earned a black eye in the process.

Evans hit 256 homers from 1980 to 1989, more than any other A.L. player during that decade. Other decade leaders were: 1900-09 Harry Davis -67;1910-19 Gavvy Cravath-116; 1920-29 Babe Ruth – 467; 1930-39 Jimmie Foxx- 415; 1940-49 Ted Williams – 234; 1950-59 Mickey Mantle – 280; 1960-69 Harmon Killebrew – 393; 1970-79 Reggie Jackson – 292; 1980-89 Dwight Evans – 256; 1990-99 Mark McGwire – 405 (mixed A.L. & N.L.).

Asked before the 1986 season to name the greatest highlight of his career in Boston thus far, Evans did not mention home runs, Golden Glove awards, or even his rifle throws to the plate to save a run. His number-one achievement? "Driving a car in Boston for 13 years without a dent."

Carl Everett

Like a nova that bursts into light and then fades, Carl Everett soared during his initial half-season with the Red Sox, even making the 2000 American League All-Star team. But then Everett crashed and burned so spectacularly that in just two years—to many fans it felt like 20—he had acquired the nickname C. Everett Kook and had earned himself a place on numerous "All-Bosox Wacko" teams.

This is not an easy list to make. With characters like Wade Boggs, Oil Can Boyd, Jimmy Piersall, Bill Lee, Ted Williams, Mickey McDermott, Sammy White, Babe Ruth . . . the list goes on and on . . . it's harder to crack than Richard Nixon's famous "enemies list." Everett did his darnedest and just may have succeeded.

Blessed with amazing natural abilities and an admirable on-field work ethic, Everett quickly won over Sox fans with anti-Yankees remarks directed at his one-time team.

His pronouncement that he didn't believe in dinosaurs because he'd never seen one earned him the nickname "Jurassic Carl."

On July 15, 2000, the far from dormant Mount Everett erupted after umpire Ron (Mea) Kulpa re-established the batter's box and told Carl to stay within it. Carl went ballistic and before the argument was over, he head-butted the umpire and earned himself a 10-day suspension. Brian Daubach took Everett's place in the lineup and hit a three-run homer to win the game.

A number of other run-ins with manager Jimy Williams, the Boston media and even well-respected fellow players like Darren Lewis and Bret Saberhagen followed. In spring training, a frustrated Williams ordered the bus to actually leave on time one day, leaving a furious Everett behind.

The straw that broke the Sox GM's faith in Everett, though, came just a few days after the September 11 attacks on the World Trade Center when Everett showed up late for a workout, got in an argument with new manager Kerrigan, called Kerrigan a "racist" and earned himself another suspension. *USA Today* columnist Mike LoPresti called Everett a "national disgrace." In a time when the American people as a whole was focused on helping heal the nation, Everett— who was being paid at the rate of roughly $43,000 per game —couldn't manage to show up for work on time and then exploded when taken to task.

Ladies and gentlemen, boys and girls, Everett has now left the building!

Sherm Feller

Sherm Feller was a public address mainstay at Fenway Park for many years, and his measured voice was one of the most distinctive and recognizable in all of New England. On one occasion, however, it was Miller time in Boston and no one even knew. Jon Miller, the talented Baltimore Orioles and ESPN broadcaster and part-time mimic, was at Fenway covering the Orioles-Red Sox series. In the course of the game, Miller, a former Red Sox broadcaster, visited Feller to renew old acquaintances. When Feller had to leave the booth briefly on a matter of some undetermined urgency, Miller stepped into the breach and didn't miss a beat. Feller did a double take when he heard himself apparently speaking in his own absence and hurried back to the booth. He was so impressed and amused that he allowed the interloper to continue announcing players for the next three innings. No one in the ballpark knew they were listening to a sham Sherm.

Rick Ferrell

On July 17, 1933, Rick Ferrell batted for Boston and faced brother Wes who was pitching for the Indians at the time. He told Dick Thompson, "In the second inning, I homered off Wes, and in the third inning, he homered off Hank Johnson. It was the first time in history that brothers homered while playing against each other in the same game.

Wes and Rick Farrell (Brace Photography)

We laughed a lot about that, though Wes was upset that I hit mine off him. He didn't like that at all."

Just what we need, a new baseball stat—the quadruple triple. In 1934, Rick Ferrell was one of four Boston players to triple, all in the same inning. Part of a 12-run inning, Ferrell was joined by Carl Reynolds, Moose Solters and Bucky Walters—all of whom tripled. In the same inning, batting around, Ferrell also walked, Reynolds singled, Solters singled and Walters doubled.

The Ferrell brothers, Wes and Rick, were part of a robust farm family of seven boys who grew up in rural North Carolina. Living on the land they used to improvise baseball games on the pastures near their house. They devised a way to record the longest hit of the day by planting a stick in the ground at the point the ball eventually landed. It became a point of some family honor to go and move the stick beyond its present place and the last, furthest stick gave the hitter bragging rights for the rest of the day. This tradition was carried over to the major leagues—sort of. On that July day, Red Sox catcher Rick Ferrell hit a home run off his brother Wes, then pitching for the Cleveland Indians. As he was circling the bases he taunted his brother with a coded message. "Hey Wes," he said, "you'd better go put up a stick for that one." Rick may have been the only other person on the field who knew what the reference meant. Wes did not take the teasing well. He became very agitated and began to kick dirt around the infield.

The family feud was fought to a draw that day however, when Wes homered in the bottom of that same inning. As he crossed the plate he had the last word for that day. "Hey Rick, looks like you're going to have to move that stick back some."

Wes Ferrell

In August of 1936, Wes Ferrell was suspended for ten days and fined $1,000 by then-manager Joe Cronin after the temperamental pitcher left the mound in a huff during a game at Yankee Stadium. Citing poor defense behind him, the 20-game winner acted like a spoiled child, throwing his glove and cap into the air and stomping from the field in front the of the amused New York crowd. He had made a similar unauthorized exit just days earlier in Boston and Cronin had seen enough.

When he found out about the fine, Ferrell was beside himself with anger. "I'm going to slug that *&%* Irishman right on his lantern jaw," he is reported to have told team-mates. Cronin was scarcely intimidated. "Fine," he told the handsome right-hander. "I want to see you when we get off the bus in the alley by the hotel." The manager was all too ready to duke it out with this malcontent; however, Ferrell failed to show up at the appointed time and place. Ferrell was an amateur astrologer and used the stars to guide his life decisions. Whatever he saw in the stars that night obviously prevented him from seeing many more stars later.

Carlton Fisk (Brace Photography)

Carlton Fisk

Neither rain nor snow nor sleet nor hail. . . . Blame it on the post office. At the end of the 1980 season, in which he stroked 18 homers and batted .289, Boston's Hall of Fame catcher Carlton Fisk was expected to re-sign with the Red Sox. When his contract was not postmarked by the deadline date, however, he was free to pursue other offers and eventually signed with the Chicago White Sox, where he continued to accumulate HOF stats until his retirement. Hired by Dan Duquette shortly before he was elected to the Hall of Fame, Fisk proudly wore his Red Sox cap during the ceremonies in Cooperstown and his #27 was retired by the Red Sox in ceremonies at Fenway later in the year.

Bill Lee was Fisk's battery-mate during much of his time in Boston and remains a close friend today. "Fisk had durability, he was tough. He was the runt of the litter of the Fisk family. His father is 87 and still cleans his flue, goes up on the roof. Fisk is the only prima donna in the bunch. It's ironic that it was all during the turmoil of Yawkey dying and Haywood [Sullivan] taking over and bringing his son [catcher Marc Sullivan] into the fold, that the Red Sox thought that Fisk was expendable. [Branch] Rickey always said that it was better to trade a player one year too early than one year too late, but in the Fisk case it turned out to be a decade too early. "

Fats Fothergill

Fats Fothergill couldn't have been *too* fat. Before he came to the Red Sox from Detroit, he hit a home run at Fenway for the Tigers, rounded the bases and did a front flip, landing right on home plate. At 5'10 1/2" he weighed 230. Kirby Puckett was 5'8" and weighed 210 but you can bet no one ever called him "Fats." At least not to his face.

Fothergill sounds like a figure to mock, but his career average after 12 years in the majors was .325. Though he broke in at 230 pounds, as his career progressed his weight began to climb towards his average. In only three of his years did he bat below .300. Floyd Conner says Fothergill once bit umpire Bill Dineen during an argument during a period when he was on a crash diet. "That was the first bite of meat I've had in a month," he explained.

Jimmie Foxx

Lefty Gomez once suggested that Foxx "wasn't scouted —he was trapped."

Cleveland Indians pitcher Lloyd Brown had had enough of Jimmie Foxx. After Foxx hit a game-winning ninth-inning home run off Brown, the frustrated pitcher decided to take direct action against the man known as "The Beast." "That's the last time you'll ever do that against me," he threatened. "Why? Are you quitting the game?" replied Foxx.

Foxx, known as "The Beast", shared some of Babe Ruth's prodigious appetites. The day before Independence Day in 1940, a lifelong Foxx fan, retired sea captain Israel Blake from Orrs Island, Maine offered Jimmie a dozen lobsters if he hit a home run in the game that day. Blake had actually brought down 18 lobsters, one for each of Foxx's home runs to that point in the season. Foxx did hit a homer and later downed all the crustaceans at one sitting.

It was actually quite a game. The Sox had been down 10-3 before clawing their way back. Jim Tabor hit a three-run homer in the eighth, but Philadelphia came right back, scoring a lone run in the top of the ninth. Boston's last ups saw them down by a score of 11-6. After two runs had scored, Ted Williams took Chubby Dean deep for a game-tying three-run homer into the A' s bullpen. Screwballer Nelson Foster was brought in and Foxx poked his second pitch into the screen just inside the left field foul pole—a walk-off home run followed by a feast fit for a beast!

When Yankees pitcher Lefty Gomez was watching Neil Armstrong's moon landing, his wife asked him what the white sphere was that the astronaut had just picked up. "That's the ball Foxx hit off me in New York in 1937," Gomez said.

Rich Garces

First came El Tiante, then the Yankees came up with El Duque. Rich Garces, from Venezuela, quickly became a true fan favorite in Boston soon after he joined the Red Sox in 1996. "El Guapo" (as he is called, a term essentially meaning in today's lingo, "the hottie") is listed as 255 pounds but most everyone realizes there's at least another 50 or more pounds on his portly 6'0" frame. He's piled up an enviable win-loss record with the Red Sox, 23-7, always in relief — a tribute to the number of times the Bosox have come from behind or broken open a tied game. As a result, "El Guapo" T shirts have become popular items in Boston.

El Guapo was the "bad guy" in the movie *Three Amigos* and the tag may have first been hung on Sr. Garces by Sean McDonough as a result, even though Garces is from Venezuela and not Mexico. One Fenway bleacher creature occasionally turns up costumed like the character in the film, in a sombrero and poncho.

In 2001, Manny Ramirez began wearing his pants so low and baggy that he looked certain to trip on them as he ran.   He said he'd begun wearing El Guapo's pants.

When Garces showed up for spring training 2002, after losing 35 pounds over the winter, bringing him down to a reported 245 pounds, he said he'd had to buy a whole new wardrobe. Some of the other Red Sox were impressed at the still-not-svelte short reliever, and when someone asked Brian Daubach if he'd seen "Guapo" yet, Dauber said, "Yeah, what's left of him."

Nomar Garciaparra

Even when he isn't hitting, Nomar has a hot bat. Ex-teammate Jeff Frye completed hitting for the cycle Friday night August 17, 2001, for the Toronto Blue Jays — hitting a gapper and holding up with a single. It actually would have been a sure double, but Frye, at the urging of the first base coach, stopped at first to complete the rare hitting feat.

The Sox link? Frye was using one of Nomar's bats. Apparently on his last trip to Fenway he asked Nomar for a couple (Nomar gave him five) as he felt they would "have some hits in them." Apparently he was right.

Nomar Garciaparra admires Derek Jeter's range and A-Rod's quickness, but his real hero is much more animated than any of those guys. "When I was a kid, I tried all the positions, and I enjoyed 'em all," he said. "Actually, catching was my favorite, because it's a position where you can be almost like a quarterback, seeing the whole field and running the game from behind the plate.

"Back then, my idol was Bugs Bunny, because I saw a cartoon of him playing ball—you know, the one where he plays every position himself with nobody else on the field but him? Now that I think of it, Bugs is still my idol. You have to love a ballplayer like that." — Nomar Garciaparra, in *Diehard.*

Rich Gedman

Red Sox fan Tim Savage, a former vendor at Fenway, writes:

"My most enduring memory of Rich Gedman was that he was involved in an incident against the Tigers that remains the most bizarre play I ever saw. Gedman was catching and Lou Whitaker was on first, when Kirk Gibson ripped a gapper. Since Whitaker had to hold up for a moment to see if it might be caught, Gibson was right on his tail as he rounded third. The throw came in, Gedman tagged out Whitaker at the plate, and umpire Larry Barnett stepped into the baseline to make the out call. As he did so, Gibson came barreling in and smashed right into Barnett, knocking him out.

"Gedman was smart enough to step out of the way, and applied the tag on Gibson as he ran by. (Third base umpire) Ken 'King Kong' Kaiser came over, and seeing a ball on the ground that had apparently fallen out of Barnett's ball bag during the collision, ruled that Gedman had dropped the ball and Gibson was safe. Ralph Houk came out to argue the call, and he and Kaiser squared off while standing over Barnett's fallen body. It reminded me of all those scenes in the *Iliad* where the Greeks and the Trojans fight over the corpse of a slain comrade."

Gary Geiger

His name may have been Geiger but he was no counter. In a 1961 game at Fenway, the Red Sox were trailing the Los Angeles Angels 3-2 in the tenth inning. Chuck Schilling worked the pitcher for a two-out walk bringing Gary Geiger to the plate. Geiger came through with a hard drive to the outfield fence for a triple, scoring Schilling with the tying run. Unfortunately Geiger thought that Schilling represented the winning run and held up between third and home. He was caught in a run-down and was tagged out.

Dick Gernert

En route to the 1958 Most Valuable Player Award, Red Sox outfielder Jackie Jensen was complaining about being in a mild slump. Roommate Dick Gernert who was mired in a real slump was unsympathetic. "I'll settle for your slumps," grumbled Gernert, who was mired in hitting quicksand.

Don Gile

Like Ted Williams, Don Gile hit a home run in his last at bat in the major leagues! Gile was on the Red Sox roster for every single game of the 1962 season—but did not get a single hit until the very last day. In fact, he sat on the bench the first 34 or so games without even making it to the plate. Then Manager Pinky Higgins put him in—against Whitey Ford, of all people! Gile struck out on four pitches.

The next time Gile was brought in to hit in a game situation, there were two outs in the ninth, and the runner got picked off. That day he played both halves of a double-header and managed only a weak single in the first. But in the eighth inning of the night-cap, he hit an eighth inning home run in his last major league at-bat. There is no report on whether or not Gile tipped his cap to the crowd.

Mike Greenwell

Greenwell broke in with a bang. His first three hits in the major leagues were all home runs. If he'd kept it up, he'd have an even 1400 home runs — and the Red Sox probably wouldn't have let him go after the 1996 season.

One Boston writer said that whenever Greenwell looked in the mirror he saw Carl Yastrzemski.

Lefty Grove

"Gimme a blank contract," Grove would ask Yawkey. "I'll sign it and you fill in the figures."

Grove had exactly 300 career wins and led the league nine times in ERA, four of them when he pitched for the Red Sox in hitter-friendly Fenway. His six shutouts in 1936 aLso led the American League.

Double or nothing?   On June 9, 1934, Lefty Grove gave up six doubles in one inning to assorted Washington Senators.

One spring in Sarasota, Lefty Grove tried to attach a firecracker to Ted Williams' auto engine, but broke a handle lifting the hood, and cut his pitching hand severely.

Creighton Gubanich

Catcher Creighton Gubanich had a brush with fame on May 2, 1999. On that day he became the first Red Sox player ever whose first major league hit was a grand slam home run. He was sent back to the minors without getting into another game. Called back up a while later, he managed 47 at bats and a .277 average but never did hit another one out.

Carroll Hardy

Want to impress a pretty girl or get a free drink at any bar in the United States of America? Just tell them you once pinch-hit for Ted Williams. Of course, you may have to have some proof like Carroll Hardy does. Hardy, who played for the Red Sox from 1960-62, is best remembered as the only man to pinch-hit for Williams. Think about that for a minute. Ted Williams was a lifetime .344 hitter with 521 home runs and a .400 season under his belt. Hardy, a career .225 hitter with 17 home runs in eight major league seasons, was like another species when it came to hitting. So how did this event come to pass, you ask?

During the last part of the 1960 season, Ted Williams came to the plate in a meaningless game in Baltimore and fouled a ball off his instep. Williams was taken out of the game and immediately returned home to Boston. Red Sox manager Pinky Higgins sent Hardy, a utility outfielder, into the game to pinch-hit for Williams. It would be nice to report that this Hardy boy was so inspired by the notion of replacing Ted that he came through with a heroic home run. Alas, he hit into a double-play to end the inning, but the event did give Hardy some pretty exclusive bragging rights. When Ted met Hardy years later he greeted him with a grin and said, "Well, I guess I made you famous."

Hardy also pinch-hit for Carl Yastrzemski, making him the only hitter to pinch-hit for two of the biggest legends in Boston sports history.

Bucky Harris

One might think managers were above practical jokes of their own, but not always. In 1934, around the Fourth of July, Red Sox manager Bucky Harris once threw a cigar with a flaming "blue nosed" match stuck in it into a Pullman washroom where a card game was in progress. Players sometimes held card games in the washroom because it was larger than the berths on the train. The match flared up and the cigar looked to the six startled players like a big firecracker. The baseball men were playing in their BVDs due to the summer heat on the long ride to St. Louis, and they played with a cardboard "table" held on their knees. When they saw what they thought was a monster firecracker tossed into the room, everything went flying — chips, cards, and the like, as the participants bolted out of that washroom as fast as they could.

Scott Hatteberg

Baseball is sometimes a game of sin and redemption — and sweet revenge. August 6, 2001— the Red Sox were leading Texas 4-2 when they had a chance to break the game wide open in the bottom of the fourth inning. Catcher Scott Hatteberg came up with runners on first and second and nobody out. Hatteberg did the worst thing he could do in this particular situation — he lined hard, right into a triple play. The Rangers promptly scored five runs in the top of the fifth, giving them a solid 7- 4 lead. In the bottom of the sixth, Hatteberg came up again with nobody out — this time with the bases loaded. Redeeming himself as well as anyone possibly could, he slammed a pitch into the Red Sox bullpen. No one had ever hit into a triple play and hit a grand slam in the same game. "From the outhouse to the penthouse," a happy Hattie said in a postgame interview.

Jim Henry

You work on this play for hours and hours in spring training and then something like this happens! On September 25, 1936 in a game between the Red Sox and Senators in Washington, Red Sox pitcher Jim Henry (career record of 6-2 with a 4.79 ERA over three ML seasons) found himself in a tight situation. The Senators were threatening to score in the bottom of the third with Joe Kuhel on third and Johnny Stone on first. Stalling for time, Henry walked behind the mound and picked up the rosin bag. While thus preoccupied, the Senators decided to pull a double steal on him. Glancing up, Henry was so surprised that he wheeled and threw the rosin bag to second base instead of the ball. Kuhel scored, Stone was safe at second, and when the dust had settled—and the laughter had subsided—the umpire ruled it a double steal. No error was charged to Henry, but just as his crimson face was returning to normal, Stone stole third on his very next pitch. Red Sox manager Joe Cronin had seen enough. He walked to the mound and sent the embarrassed pitcher to the showers—where presumably he threw in the towel.

John Henry

In February 2002, while waiting for the I's to be dotted and the T's crossed on his group's purchase of the Red Sox, new principal owner John Henry pulled up in a huge Florida Marlins bus at The Plantation Inn in Crystal River,

Florida for the Ted Williams Hitters Hall of Fame dinner and induction ceremonies. Henry had sold the Marlins team less than 12 hours earlier, but explained he'd arranged to borrow the bus through the end of spring training so he could commute from his home in Boca Raton to the Red Sox spring training site in Fort Myers.

Henry got out of the Marlins bus all by himself—he was the only passenger—and carried his own overnight case and garment bag, walked down the drive and checked into the hotel without any retinue. Dressed in jeans and a light sweater, slight of stature, the unassuming owner probably wouldn't have known what to make of Roger Clemens' complaints that Red Sox players had to carry their own luggage —but the private bus idea is scary. Twenty-five players—25 buses?

Mike Herrera

Were the Red Sox the last major league team to sign a black player? Or were they one of the first? Did the Red Sox actually have a black ballplayer long before Pumpsie Green and 22 years before Jackie Robinson debuted with the Dodgers? Cuba's Ramon "Mike" Herrera totaled 276 at bats in 1925 and 1926 while serving as a second baseman for the Red Sox (an even .275 batting average). He also played for Negro League teams both before and after his stretch with Boston.

Before joining the Red Sox, Herrera had played for Almendares in Havana, as well as with La Union, all Leagues and the (Cuban) Red Sox. The Boston Red Sox purchased him from their Springfield (Eastern League) club. The *Bos-*

ton Globe termed him a "splendid prospect" and he did go 2 for 5 in his first game.

Todd Bolton, asked about Herrera's history in the Negro Leagues, replied:

"In the pre-Negro League years he barnstormed in the U.S. with the Long Branch Cubans and the Jersey City Cubans. When the first Negro National League was formed in 1920 Herrera was a member of the Cuban Stars (West), one of the inaugural teams in the league. He stayed on with the team in 1921 when it became the Cincinnati Cubans. Herrera returned to the Negro Leagues for one final season in 1928 with Alejandro Pompez' Cuban Stars (East).

Photographs of Mike Herrera seem to show that he could easily "pass" for white, and for those who want to measure such things, he may have been more white than black. So did he have to "pass for black" when he was in the Negro Leagues? Not really, Bolton explains. There were a number of light-skinned players in the Negro Leagues and even "white" Cubans. These players were used to playing together in Latin America. It was only in the United States that they were segregated.

Harry Hooper

Harry Hooper is said to be the first American League player to make use of flip-down sunglasses. He was also one of the first to employ the sliding catch that has become such a common part of today's game. Hooper was a threat at the plate and on the base paths, stealing a total of 300 bases for the Sox and another 75 for the Chicago White Sox.

Harry Hooper (Brace Photography)

Considered by many to be the greatest defensive right fielder in the history of the game, Hooper, along with teammates Tris Speaker and Duffy Lewis comprised the best outfield in baseball. No less an authority than Walter Johnson called Hooper "the toughest out of all in a pinch."

When Hooper homered in the ninth inning of the fifth and final game of the 1915 World Series, it was the first time a Series had ever been decided by the long ball. Hooper actually hit two homers in that final game, the first breaking a 4-4 tie.

It was also Hooper who argued that Babe Ruth would be more valuable if he played every day in the outfield rather that just pitching every forth or fifth day. His argument was not accepted at first, but eventually agreed to when Hooper pointed out how crowds increased every time Ruth played. Hooper was placed in charge of teaching Ruth the outfield. Hooper took over center when Ruth was learning the ropes in right.

Hooper was the only Red Sox player to play on all four World Championship teams—1912, 1914, 1915 and 1918.

Tex Hughson

Some men dream of shapely women, but others dream of different kinds of curves. Tex Hughson talked in his sleep and roomie Boo Ferriss said that he would go over every pitch he threw, adding comments on what (in some cases) he should have thrown.

Bruce Hurst

Before Roger Clemens brought his fastball and winning ways to Boston, the Red Sox pitching staff got about as much respect as Rodney Dangerfield. The Red Sox teams of the late seventies and early eighties were blessed with great offensive players like Yaz, Wade Boggs, Jim Rice, and Dwight Evans to name just a few. Bosox pitchers were invariably blamed for the Red Sox's lack of success—sometimes with reason. Bruce Hurst, Bob Ojeda and John Tudor were all talented pitchers, but their confidence was somewhat shaken when a Boston newspaper referred to the trio as "Plague, Pestilence and Death." Hurst credits the arrival of Rocket Roger for changing all that.

I Iurst felt so strongly about Clemens that when Roger got into an argument with an umpire at first base in 1986, Hurst hustled out of the dugout to defend his teammate and he wound up being ejected. The umpire said that Hurst used a profanity. Hurst is a devout Mormon and does not curse. 'That is one of the most ridiculous things I've ever heard,' Roger said at the time. 'He might have said, "gosh darn."'

Pete Jablonowski

Pete Jablonowski was one of those hurlers who didn't exactly shine with the Red Sox. In 1932, he went 0-3 with the Sox after coming over from the Indians. With the exception of pitching two innings for the Yankees in 1933, he was out of the majors until he reappeared in 1936 with the Senators, having changed his name to Pete Appleton. That one year, freshly named, he went 14-9 with a 3.53 ERA, but then returned to his formal level of mediocrity, ending his career with a 57-66 record. Perhaps he should have changed his name a second time—to Feller.

Jackie Jensen

It has been said that Jackie Jensen was one-third of the most high-strung outfield in baseball history. It's a claim that's difficult to dispute. Jensen, who feared flying, was in right, Ted Williams was in left and Jimmy Piersall in center.

Jensen was a three-time A.L. RBI champ—in 1955, 1958 and 1959. Like many Red Sox stars before and since, Jensen was often the target for heckling and verbal abuse from the Fenway fans. The boos and catcalls bothered the sensitive outfielder more than he was willing to admit, despite the fact that most Red Sox fans were 100 percent in his corner. Jensen once described the science of crowd reaction. "Boos sound louder than cheers," he explained. "One boo carries a long way. Twenty or thirty can sound like the whole ballpark."

After his MVP season in 1958, the boos were replaced by cheers, and Jensen suddenly could do no wrong. Once in a game with the Baltimore Orioles, Jensen missed a pitch by a country mile. In earlier times this would have brought loud jeers from all corners of Fenway Park. Now there were only words of encouragement. When Jensen stepped out of the batter's box to collect his thoughts for the next pitch, Orioles catcher Gus Triandos said very quietly, "Boo!" Jensen immediately saw the humor in the situation. "Thanks, Gus, that makes me feel at home." Thus relaxed, he promptly hit the next delivery over the Green Monster.

Jensen almost stole Ted Williams' biggest act. In 1959, while Ted was struggling through his worst major league season, Jensen was having another banner year. He was terribly homesick for his family, however, and still had a dreadful fear of flying. In August he announced that the '59 season might be his last. Because the Red Sox were well out of the pennant race, Jensen asked for permission to end his season one day early in order to return to his loved ones on the west coast.

His last game was a Saturday contest against the Washington Senators at Fenway Park. Jensen was battling Cleveland slugger Rocky Colavito for the A.L. RBI title. Coming to the plate in the bottom of the ninth with the Senators leading 4-2, he was trailing Colavito by two ribbies. With the bases loaded, Jensen doubled to left and a fan touched the ball, creating a ground-rule double that drove in two runs to tie the game and draw even with "The Rock". Then in the 11th inning, with two men out, Jensen hit a dramatic homer to win the game.

Colavito didn't drive in any runs that day. Jensen was up by one RBI — and he went home instead of playing the final game, saying, "It doesn't mean enough to me. I've had enough chances already. If we were fighting for fourth place, I'd stay." Colavito did play but again failed to drive in a run and thus Jensen won the American League RBI championship. There was a buzz in the press box as writers mumbled about the possible great exit that the homer represented if Jensen indeed decided to retire. Jensen did retire — at least for the entire 1960 season — only to return for one last season in 1961. His final at bat came in the eighth inning of the final game. It was the game in which Tracy Stallard yielded Roger Maris' 61st home run. Jensen pinch-hit for Stallard and popped up. Boston lost 1-0.

In 1954 when Jackie Jensen was traded from the Washington Senators to the Boston Red Sox for Mickey McDermott and Tom Umphlett, he reacted with uncharacteristic enthusiasm. "How do I like the trade? How do I like apple pie—duck soup—making a million dollars? Boy, I love the trade!"

John Kennedy

John Kennedy was honored by the Boston Baseball Writers Association for his versatility in filling in at second, third and shortstop—as well as for his timely hitting. Known as "Super Sub," the infielder with the presidential sounding name was playing in the right part of the country. When he was just three years old, his father was playing marbles with him on the living room floor. FDR had just died and the elder Kennedy asked John if he wanted to be president some day. "No, I want to be a ballplayer," the youngster replied, a fact his father entered into his baby book for posterity.

From 1962 through 1974, JK played for six teams, winding up his career with four seasons in Boston. Rumor has it that like the president, he also lived in a white house, vacationed in Hyannisport, and once said, "Ask not what the Red Sox can do for you, ask what you can do for the Red Sox."

Kennedy hit an inside-the-park HR his first time up as a Red Sox rookie.

Kevin Kennedy

The only player on both teams who did not play in Pawtucket's "Longest Game" was with the Orioles' Rochester Red Wings team at the time. It was Kevin Kennedy, later Red Sox manager and currently a Fox Sports TV commentator. This 33-inning game took 67 days to complete—it started on April 18, 1981 and ended on June 23, 1981. Actual playing time was eight hours and 25 minutes. Pitch count for Pawsox pitchers: 459. Pawsox hurlers struck out 34. Quite a number of major league ballplayers of note participated in the contest: for the Red Sox, Marty Barrett, Wade Boggs, Sam Bowen, Rich Gedman, Lee Graham, Roger LaFrancois, Julio Valdez, and Chico Walker all saw action; as did pitchers Luis Aponte, Joel Finch, Bruce Hurst, Bobby Ojeda, Win Remmerswaal, and Mike Smithson. Manny Sarmiento pitched for the Pawsox, but never made it to the Boston team, though he did spend parts of seven seasons in the big leagues. A prospect named Cal Ripken played third base for Rochester and went 2 for 13. Kevin Kennedy sat on the bench, maybe hoping for a pinch-hitting role if the innings reached the high 30s. During the game he had a lot of time to contemplate his future, no doubt concluding that if you can't get playing time in a 33-inning game, it may well be time to hang up the old spikes and turn to managing.

Marty Keough

How tough are Boston fans? In spring training 1960, Marty Keough was in a car crash that occurred well after curfew. The saying of the day was "Keough can't hit a curve with an automobile."

Henry Killilea

Killilea was the owner of the Boston Pilgrims, forerunners of the modern day Red Sox. The Pilgrims won the first modern World Series featuring the A.L. champion Pilgrims against the Pittsburgh Pirates, the best of the National League. The Pilgrims won the eight-game marathon, becoming the first World Series champion. Cy Young even pitched in while not on the mound, helping sell tickets before the game. The Pilgrims lost a few public relations points, though, when Pirate owner Barney Dreyfuss was forced to pay his way into the Boston ballpark.

Wendell Kim

The Red Sox have rarely been considered fleet afoot. Small wonder then that when late 1990s third base coach Wendell Kim sprinted across the diamond on the way to take his position, beating every Sox fielder out, some considered him the fastest runner on the team. Not surprisingly, Fenway crowds used to greet his mad dashes with appreciative applause.

Wendell Kim always enjoyed showing off his magic tricks at the beginning of the season and he was really quite good. His abilities even got him hired for professional engagements as a magician. Perhaps the popular Kim's biggest disappearing act was his quick exit from the Red Sox coaching staff after some highly questionable third base coaching decisions during the 2000 season.

Ellis Kinder

"Ellis Kinder was our closer," recalls former Sox teammate Billy Consolo. "That man was a man's man! He was the strongest human being. He was scared of nothing. He used to show up about the seventh inning and go to the bullpen. He knew he wasn't going to be playing until the eighth or ninth inning. That's the kind of man he was."

Mickey McDermott was Kinder's teammate and drinking partner. "Kinder didn't know what water was," says McDermott. "He thought the Atlantic Ocean was a chaser. They said drink Canada Dry and he tried to do it."

"Old Folks," as Kinder was sometimes known, may have thought he was hallucinating, but it really happened: while he was on the mound at Fenway Park, a passing seagull dropped a smelt on him.

Kinder pitched under Red Sox manager Joe Cronin. Maureen Cronin recalls her father's frustration with the talented but undisciplined pitcher. "I can't imagine being a batter and knowing the pitcher is drunk as a skunk and you trying to hit the ball. He was bombed while he was out there. I can't imagine anything worse. Can you imagine facing Roger Clemens or Randy Johnson after they'd had a couple of pops? Dad tried not to say bad things about people and when I asked him to write a book, he said he couldn't really say all the things he knew."

Ellis Kinder

Roger LaFrancois

The last man to play with a major league club for an entire season and hit .400 was not Ted Williams, but a fellow Red Soxer, Roger LaFrancois. Roger used to go to Red Sox games as a kid. He signed with the Red Sox and came up in their system, even receiving instruction from Ted Williams during spring training at Winter Haven. In 1982, it all paid off. Roger made the club out of spring training as a backup catcher behind Gary Allenson and Rich Gedman and he spent the full 162-game season with the Red Sox, making every homestand and every road trip. He didn't miss a game.

Unfortunately, he also didn't get to play in that many of them. The first time he appeared in a game was May 27, and by that time the Boston papers had already begun to run photos of him with captions such as "Day 32: do you know who this man is?" Ralph Houk was from the old school and as, LaFrancois says, "played nine". He really didn't utilize his bench the way managers do today. LaFrancois appeared only very briefly and approaching the final day of the season had only been in seven games, with five at bats and only a double and a single to show for it. Still, he was batting .400.

Then Houk gave him the opportunity to start the game, and Roger faced a dilemma like the young Ted Williams faced in 1941. Should he sit out the game and preserve his .400 average, or should he go for it? "There was a lot of pressure on me that last day, but I didn't want to sit on my average," Roger quips today. "I decided to play." It turned out to be an 11-inning affair against the Yankees in the Stadium. Roger hit a solid single up the middle earlier in the game but then saw his average sink to .333 as the game went into extra innings and he'd gone 1 for 4. In the top of the 11th, though, the young catcher jumped on a 1-2 Rudy May breaking ball and bounced it over the pitcher's head for an infield hit. Three batters later, LaFrancois scored what proved to be the winning run on a Rick Miller single. His average stands in the record books at an even .400 today.

Roger LaFrancois is now the hitting coach with the Binghamton Double A team in the New York Mets system.

Roger LaFrancois is perhaps the only ballplayer to play on the same team as his childhood idol, Carl Yastrzemski, and also his idol's son. LaFrancois played with Yaz on the Boston Red Sox in 1982 and with Michael Yastrzemski on the Durham ballclub in the Atlanta Braves system.

Bill Lee

Lee won 17 games three years in a row, 1973 through 1975. He also was a self-appointed and outspoken social critic of sorts, a constant source of amusement who garnered attention and applause from Boston's left-leaning college crowd. When he termed Boston a "racist city" (by no means was he the first to do so), equally outspoken City Councilor Albert "Dapper" O'Neil fired off a letter. "Dapper" spelled several words incorrectly, giving Spaceman the opening to write back a polite letter advising the councilor that some semi-literate idiot had gotten possession of his

Bill Lee

stationery and was writing embarrassing letters over his name.

When asked by a *Boston Globe* reporter "what is your role with the Red Sox?" The Spaceman replied, "I'm George Scott's interpreter!"

Lee wore number 37 during his time with the Red Sox, but would have preferred number 337. "That way," he explained, " if I stood on my head people would know who I am."

An envious Bill Lee once pointed out that Tibetan priests had the ability to make a baseball disappear and then reappear in the catcher's mitt. "There's my idea of an ideal relief pitcher," he said.

Lee used the English language to paint some vivid if abstract images. After the Red Sox defeated the Oakland A's, he said that the A's were "emotionally mediocre, like Gates Brown sleeping on a rug." Huh?

Lee ran for president of the United States on the farcical Rhinoceros Party ticket. He was asked for his position on the highly controversial issue of drug testing in baseball: "My position on mandatory drug testing? I've tested mescaline. I've tested 'em all. But I don't think it should be mandatory."

When a young Bill Lee first visited Fenway Park and looked out to left field, he could scarcely believe his eyes.

For southpaws, having the Green Monster just 310' away is about as reassuring as having a buzzard perched on your shoulder. Ever the optimist, Lee thought that the Wall might all be some temporary structure. "Do they leave it there during the game?" he asked hopefully.

Bill Lee and Carlton Fisk were a very effective battery for the Red Sox and they remain close friends. Nevertheless, they didn't always see eye to eye.

"I came up with Fisk, and he always thought he was the team leader. I wouldn't let him get away with that. I liked his attitude, but I knew I was smarter than him. He was tough as nails. We got along well but we were like brothers—we fought a lot, like in all sibling rivalries—about the way to handle the game and pitch to certain batters. He was more of a challenger and I was more of a nibbler. I would change up when he wouldn't expect it and he'd get really mad and throw the ball back at me hard. I made some mistakes. I'd hang a change-up in bad situations and he'd say 'I told you so'. When I made a bad pitch, it hurt me and not only did I have to suffer the direct consequences but I also had to suffer the wrath of Zimmer and the wrath of Fisk. I liked to experiment and baseball doesn't like experimentation."

Does Lee like the Spaceman label? "At first I didn't like it," he admits. "I'm not a spaceman, I'm more earth-oriented, very conservative toward the planet and liberal toward humanity. I'm so far left that I'm right. I'm a south-paw. My hand points to the south. We're laid out this way. I praise the powers that be that made me left-handed and that made me think the way that I do because I can always look in the mirror in the morning and say when things are going wrong around the earth, *Hey, it's not my fault.* You see, I'm an anarchist. I believe in pulling down boundaries and borders. I don't believe in the word sovereignty; I believe it should be stricken from the American language. I think what race, what color, what religion, what nationality you are—these are all obsolete terms in the 21st century. That's why I am the spaceman because I believe in open space."

Spaceman Communications:

"When I left Boston I said they'd find me floating face down in the Charles River with 11 stab wounds in my back and they'd say they were self-inflicted."

"Fenway Park is a shrine, but domed stadiums are sacrilegious. Playing in the Astrodome was like playing in an old pair of Adidas sneakers."

"I'd be a great manager but major league baseball has never forgiven me. If I came in I'd look like John Brown, the guy they hung at Harper's Ferry. Fire in my eyes, my hair is long and my beard goes all the way down to my navel. They'd say, 'Who the hell is this guy, the lord of the rings?' And I'd say, "That's right, boys, if you play for me you'll all have rings—some in your noses."

"The Red Sox were a Greek tragedy in the 2001 season. Pedro's arm fell off a few days after he made the comment about digging up the Babe."

"I hope the Red Sox come back next year in great shape and with new ownership. I'll be the general manager and

Stephen King will be the owner and Laurie Cabot [a Massachusetts witch] will be my pitching coach. It'll be a *real* horror show. We'll do just fine. Luis Tiant will be my third base coach, with the cigar in his mouth doing the signs and the whole bit. Bernie Carbo would be back for the Bible meetings on Sunday."

"Frank Howard hit the hardest ball off me at Fenway. It probably one-hopped a flatbed truck and went to Pittsfield."

"I'm still playing competitive baseball but everyone I know from the Red Sox are either in rehab or smoking Marlboro Lights and drinking Diet Pepsi. I've got no friends anymore. I'm the only hippie-head esoteric thinker left."

Lee once ran for president of the United States on the Rhinoceros Party ticket. When told that he was considered eccentric—if not downright goofy—the former southpaw pitcher retorted that he was normal and it was the "northpaws" who were not.

Sang-Hoon Lee

Another Spaceman may have landed, at least briefly, at Fenway. Has Bill Lee, a practicing Buddhist, been reincarnated—while he's still alive—as his namesake, Korean lefthander Sang-Hoon Lee?

"Bill Lee was crazy. So am I," said the long-haired (orange colored tresses) Lee. Sang-Hoon Lee is nicknamed

"Samson," and Red Sox GM Dan Duquette actually said in introducing him, "We think that with his long, flowing hair, he will be a good complement to Rod Beck in our bullpen."

Introduced to the media, Lee took the mound at Fenway Park early in 2000 and pretended to throw a few pitches over the plate for the benefit of photographers. The first "pitch" was apparently smashed high over the Green Monster, to see Lee's pantomimed look of distress as he followed the flight of the imaginary homer. Lee bowed to the Wall. On the second pitch, he quickly and playfully gripped his shoulder, faking an injury. As far as we know, he has yet to call his manager a gerbil or sprinkle foreign substances on his pancakes.

Lee was the first player to see duty in three different countries playing professional baseball: Korea, Japan and the USA.

Dutch Leonard

Hubert Benjamin "Dutch" Leonard pitched six years for Boston, including a stupendous 19-5 season in 1914, with a 0.96 ERA—the best ever in the 20th century. After six seasons with the Red Sox, his *highest* earned run average was 2.72. When sold to the Yankees by Frazee, he refused to pitch unless he was paid the full year's salary in advance. He never pitched for the Yankees; New York owner Ruppert was offended and sold him onwards to the Tigers.

Leonard must not have had a very good move to the plate. In the 15th inning of a 5-5 tie in 1913, three Cleveland players in a row stole home.

On June 20, 1918, Leonard suddenly quit the team and took a job at the Fore River Shipyard in Quincy, Massachusetts, where he proceeded to pitch for the shipyard ball team. At the close of the season, Leonard was shipped out (by the Red Sox, not by Fore River.)

This wasn't the only mid-season career switch the Sox suffered. A couple of weeks after Leonard's move, Babe Ruth let it be known he was skipping the team to play for the Bethlehem Steel Company team in Chester, Pennsylvania. Ruth relented quickly, though, and returned, helping lead the Red Sox to their last World Championship. Otherwise, who knows, he might have been sold to U.S. Steel instead of the New York Yankees and . . . well, we guess U.S. Steel would have won all those World Series instead of the Yankees.

Ted Lewis

Edward Morgan (Ted) Lewis (1872-1936), pitched for the Boston Nationals in the late 1890s and for the 1901 Red Sox (then the Pilgrims) before quitting baseball at the age of 29 and becoming a professor of English at Columbia University. He later served as president of Massachusetts State College and then as president of the University of New Hampshire. "Parson" Lewis—born in Wales—was a good friend of Robert Frost, who was quite a baseball fan himself. It's said that the two "discussed poetry and played catch in Lewis' backyard." We are not sure if it was Frost or Yogi Berra who first said "When you come to a fork in the road, take it."

Dick Littlefield

Littlefield began his career with Boston in 1950 winning two and losing two but with a 9.26 ERA. In 1951 he was with the White Sox. In 1952, the Tigers. In 1953, he pitched for the St. Louis Browns. In 1954, he appeared in three games for Baltimore. Moving over to the National League, Littlefield was with the Pirates in 1955. In 1956 he played with the Cardinals and the Giants, after opening the season with Pittsburgh. Little wonder Littlefield was dubbed the "Marco Polo of Baseball."

Jim Lonborg

Gentleman Jim Lonborg was the ace of the Red Sox pitching staff during the 1967 pennant year. The stylish right-hander won 22 games that season and became the first Boston pitcher ever to capture the Cy Young Award. Blessed with a blazing fastball and pinpoint control, he struck out 246 opposing batters in anchoring the Red Sox staff.

Before the last game of the '67 season, with the pennant still very much up for grabs, Lonborg showed that he was not immune to superstition. Since he had been more successful on the road than at Fenway during the season, he decided to check into a Boston hotel to simulate the feeling that he was on the road. He says that he fell asleep reading *The Fall of Japan,* woke refreshed in the morning, and then proceeded to defeat the Minnesota Twins to bring the pennant back to Boston for the first time in 21 years.

Larry Lucchino

Larry Lucchino, named in December 2001 as the new President of the Boston Red Sox, tells how famous Washington attorney Edward Bennett Williams gave him his entry into baseball. Williams was the owner of both the Baltimore Orioles and the Washington Redskins football team. He brought in the young Lucchino, a lawyer who'd worked with a number of attorneys, including Hillary Rodham Clinton, while with Williams' firm during the Watergate hearings. Lucchino remembers, "Edward Williams used to say to me, 'I love the Redskins, I'm crazy about the Orioles, but I'd take both of them and trade them for the Red Sox.' That's not made up. That's absolutely so. And I said, 'Of course, you're from Hartford.'"

Lucchino had strong Boston area ties before coming to the Red Sox. In 1985, when vice president of the Orioles, he was diagnosed with non-Hodgkin's lymphoma and he spent over five weeks at the Dana-Farber Cancer Institute undergoing an experimental (and clearly successful) bone marrow transplant that saved his life.

As President of the San Diego Padres, Larry and the Padres launched the Cindy Matters Fund, named for a youngster in the area who was afflicted with cancer. A couple of years ago, he told one of the authors of this book that he was very impressed with the work in pediatric oncology that he had observed at the Jimmy Fund, and he knew of the Red Sox/Ted Williams connection. "As a baseball person, I was very proud of it, so proud of it that we imitate it shamelessly out here in San Diego."

One suspects the Jimmy Fund will continue to be a favored charity of the Boston Red Sox as it has been for nearly a full half-century.

Fred Lynn

In June of 1975, his rookie season, Red Sox centerfielder Freddie Lynn drove in 10 runs in one game. He hit three homers, a triple and a single in a 15-1 win over the Detroit Tigers. His first home run came in the first inning with one man aboard; the second was a three-run job in the second, and the third came in the ninth—another three-run shot. The 16 total bases that he amassed that day tied the American League mark. Lynn went on to become the first major leaguer in history to win the Most Valuable Player Award and the Rookie of the Year in the same season! He finished with 21 homers, 105 RBIs and a .331 batting mark.

One year during the off-season, Lynn jokingly told a Los Angeles newspaper that he thought Jim Rice should be

Fred Lynn (Brace Photography)

playing leftfield because he was sick of covering up for Yaz. Many readers took the statement seriously. Next season in Chicago, Yastrzemski came all the way into Lynn's territory to make a diving catch of a sinking liner. "Showoff, " said Lynn. "Someone's gotta cover your territory, Freddie," replied a grinning Yaz.

Steve Lyons

Talk about the glamour of the Big Leagues. For a lot of his career, Lyons says, "I sat on the bench for most of the games and stared at gross puddles of chew-spit, sunflower seeds, and empty Gatorade cups all over the floor of the dug-out."

Steve Lyons played for the Red Sox in four different stints, where he gained notoriety in eating seeds and other heroic deeds. He is the only player in Red Sox history to play all nine positions and DH. He's one of only three players in major league history to play all nine positions in a game. He also claims the world's record for eating sunflower seeds in one game: five bags of David's Sunflower Seeds. But that was in Montreal, so we guess it's the National League record.

Lyons was traded from Boston to Montreal for Tom Seaver, but was then traded back for nothing. "The deal was probably that Duquette (GM for Expos at the time) would buy the next lunch when he and Red Sox General Manager Lou Gorman got together."

Sam Malone

He had Mickey McDermott's drinking habits, Bill Lee's wit, Mike Torrez' hair, Dennis Eckersley's sex appeal, and Heathcliff Slocumb's arm.

Everyone may know his name, but Sam "Mayday" Malone did not actually play for the Boston Red Sox. Nevertheless, the character portrayed so convincingly by Ted Danson on *Cheers* fits well into the Red Sox mystique— and if he didn't actually exist, he probably should have. His antics are not that much more outrageous than those of McDermott or the Spaceman, after all.

Sports Illustrated's Steve Rushin once did a straight-faced story (*SI*, May 24, 1993) about Malone in which his life was described in great detail and his entry in *The Baseball Encyclopedia* was re-produced in all its gory detail. (He is wedged in between Chuck Malone and Charlie Maloney). According to this source, Malone's career marks are not overly impressive. Born on May 1, 1948 (thus the nickname Mayday) in Sudbury, Massachusetts, the 6'3" 195-pound right-handed reliever played seven seasons with the Red Sox from 1972-1978. His record was 16 wins and 30 losses and he sports a 4.01 ERA.

Also included in the article was a "cover" from June 28, 1976 showing Mayday on the mound watching the ball exit the ballpark over the Green Monster. The caption reads

"WHAM, BAM, THANK YOU SAM: Mayday Malone Watches Another One Fly Out of Fenway." Other pictures show him in the company of Carl Yastrzemski and fictional Coach ("I always thought they gave me that name because I never flew first class") Ernie Pantusso. He missed the 1975 World Series entirely, reports *SI* due to a "mysterious domestic groin injury."

Malone had a drinking problem that may have hampered his career significantly. He admitted to having hung out too many nights at the Eliot Lounge on Mass. Ave., presumably with Bill Lee. He even admitted to occasionally drinking during games. "Never on the mound," he quickly added. "It sets a bad example for the catchers." He was also a ladies man of great repute and his pitches in that department were much more effective than those from the mound. "The closest I've ever come to saying no to a woman," he once admitted, "is 'Not now, we're landing.'" *SI* claims that Sam once requested that the Red Sox install Call Waiting in the bullpen to advance his love life. Red Sox manager Don Zimmer, never a friend of pitchers, was not amused.

Malone's pitching staple was something called "the slider of death." The name was given to the pitch by teammates who were accustomed to watching it fly out of Fenway, mortally wounding the Red Sox hopes of victory. Yankees slugger Dutch Kinkaid homered against Sam every time he faced him.

In fact, Malone surrendered many tape-measure home runs, including one that almost punched out the "O" in the CITGO sign and another, in Memorial Stadium in Baltimore, which cleared the ballpark and landed in the parking lot, where a plaque marked the spot until the park was demolished.

Sam's sole moment of glory came in September of 1972, his rookie year. In his first mound appearance in a Red Sox uniform, Malone saved both ends of a crucial double-header against the Baltimore Orioles, throwing only seven pitches to seal the two victories. Both times, Orioles slugger Boog Powell was his final out. Fenway went wild and Sam was now "Mayday" Malone.

Sports Illustrated reported that Malone's last appearance in the major leagues came in April of 1978 in Cleveland. It was his only starting assignment. The Indians' Paul Dade doubled, Larvell Blanks walked, and then Sam gave up "back-to-back-to-back-to-back homers to Andre Thornton, Buddy Bell, Willie Horton, and John Grubb." Rattled, Sam then beaned Duane Kuiper before manager Don Zimmer made his trek to the mound. This, claims *Sports Illustrated*, explains why Sammy's ERA for 1978 is represented in *The Baseball Encyclopedia* by the sideways 8, the symbol for infinity.

After his baseball career, Sam decided to open a bar and the rest, of course, is history. His friends at Cheers remained in awe of the big guy though, as much for his sexual exploits as for his baseball skills. Norm Peterson, the bar's most loyal patron, summed it up nicely: "Next to Sammy's life, my life looks dull," he said, pausing for a sip before adding, "Next to a barnacle's life, my life looks dull."

Malone did little to refute Ted Williams' assertion that all pitchers are stupid. He once said that PBS was his favorite network and that he especially liked the "two guys who talk about the day's events."

"McNeil and Lehrer?" he is asked. "No," Malone replied, "Bert and Ernie. . . . Wait a minute. Unless—maybe that's their last names."

Still Mayday could show glimmers of great intelligence. Cliff Clavin once asked him if he had the usual ballplayer superstitions. He replied, "Yeah, I had a crazy little one. I never pitched to anyone named Reggie, Willie or the Bull."

In 1992, Sam, age 43, tried a comeback with the New Britain Red Sox, Boston's Double A affiliate. Norm Peterson was excited about the prospect of Sam's return. "Boy-oh-boy," he said. "The thought of Sammy out there on the mound, chuckin' 'em down. What I wouldn't give to see that, huh?" When Cliff Clavin pointed out that New Britain was only a $30.00 train ride away, Norm replied, "Well, that's what I wouldn't give."

Sam once tried his hand at sports announcing, anchoring a local supper-hour sportscast. In a desperate attempt to attract a younger audience, he tried rapping a sports item, the final line ending, unforgettably, with the words, "G-G-G-G-G-groin injury."

The Boston Red Sox retired Sam Malone's #20 jersey in a private ceremony and it rests today in a glass display case in The 600 Club at Fenway Park. Well, semi-retired it at least. They continue to let players use the number—witness Darren Lewis in recent years. Nevertheless, on a team with characters like McDermott, Lee, Piersall, Tiant, and Conley, the name Sam Malone fits in very nicely.

Pedro Martinez

Ask major league hitters and they'll all confirm that the prospect of Pedro Martinez improving is too awful to contemplate. In the 2000 season (he was injured for much of the 2001 season), Martinez won 18 games, lost six, compiled a league-leading ERA of 1.74, almost a full two runs lower than the runner-up in the American League pitching ranks. He allowed just 42 earned runs in 217 innings of work, walked only 32 and held opponents to a puny .167 batting average, with a league-best 284 strikeouts. He captured his second consecutive Cy Young Award, winning all 28 first-place votes cast by the Baseball Writers Association of America. He also led the league in shutouts with four. Martinez is the first A.L. pitcher in history to win two consecutive Cy Youngs unanimously. He also won a Cy Young Award in the National League in '97 as a member of the Montreal Expos.

When Martinez first signed with the Dodgers, the 16 year old was 5'8" and weighed 120 pounds.

Martinez had a disastrous encounter with the baseball gods on August 29, 2000, as Pedro had a no-hitter against the Devil Rays going into the ninth. Baseball fans around the country had a chance to watch the final inning as ESPN broke into its regular programming to pick up the game feed. After a few pitches to former Red Sox catcher John Flaherty, the chain on a religious medal he was wearing around his neck snapped and Pedro tucked it in his back pocket. The very next pitch—bam! A clean single. Pedro's no-hit bid was finished.

There are signs that Pedro might be getting a tad tired of all the defeatist talk around Boston. He was once heard to observe, "One of these days Buckner's gonna catch that grounder." Apparently he's as sick as the rest of us of seeing that replay over and over.

Don't mess with the Curse of the Bambino. At least that would seem to be the message delivered to Pedro Martinez by the angered baseball gods during the 2001 baseball season. Frustrated by the never-ending talk of the supposed curse placed on the Red Sox by a departing Babe Ruth, Pedro blurted out the following: "I don't believe in damn curses. Wake up the damn Bambino and have him face me. Maybe I'll drill him in the ass." To put this outburst in further context, the statement was made by Martinez on May 30, 2001, after he had broken out of a five-game winless spell with a brilliant 3-0 performance against the Bronx Bombers. A reporter's reference to the Babe was the straw that broke the camel's back.

Was Pedro tempting Fate when he made the remark? Is God a Yankee fan as Mickey McDermott has suggested elsewhere in this book? When Pedro opened his mouth, the Red Sox, playing without superstar shortstop Nomar Garciaparra, had a record of 28-22, putting them in a virtual tie with the Yankees for first place in the A.L. East. Pedro had a record of 7-1 and Manny Ramirez was hitting as if he were playing Tee-Ball. Everything looked rosy for the Boston side. Let's consider what happened after. By mid-August the Red Sox had fallen six games out of first place and their wild-card lead had collapsed like—well, like a deck of wild cards. The Red Sox fired manager Jimy Williams who was a manager of the year candidate everywhere but in Boston. And they chose to fire him on the 53rd anniversary of the death of Babe Ruth. The Red Sox proceeded to lose their next seven consecutive games against Babe's Yankees.

Most importantly, Pedro, who was 7-1 with a 1.44 ERA on May 30, fell lower than the Babe's belly. After his controversial remarks, he suffered a rotator cuff injury and was only able to start seven more times, failing to win another game all year long. During this stretch as a mortal, his ERA ballooned to 4.54 (although his season ERA was still a brilliant 2.39.) Just to put this in perspective, Martinez had not gone seven games without a win since the first seven games of his career.

When pitching coach Joe Kerrigan took over, his first words were, "It's one of the best jobs in sports for me to be able to come in here and chase away The Curse. I look forward to the challenge." Just don't knock the Babe, Joe.

Carl Mays

Ray Collins (1914) and Carl Mays (1919) both won two games in a single day. This is the same Carl Mays who killed Ray Chapman with a beanball after he was traded to the Yankees.

The Red Sox lost a lot of games to the Detroit Tigers in 1915, and manager Rough Carrigan asked his pitching staff who among them thought he could defeat the Tigers. Carl Mays declared that if he didn't win the ball game in Detroit, he'd walk back home to Boston. He won, on his own hit, 2-1 in the ninth inning, thereby saving considerable wear and tear on his spikes.

Mickey McDermott

"Bob Neiman could hit me with the lights out," recalls McDermott. "His first two at-bats in the major leagues he hit homers off me. You could throw .306 bullets up there and he'd hit them, especially if you were a leftie. I went to Washington and we were good friends so we went out to dinner and he said, 'Tomorrow I'm going two for three off you'. I said, 'No, you're not!', and we bet $100 on it. First time up, I hit him right in the kneecap and then went into the clubhouse while he was in the whirlpool and took the $100 right out of his wallet while he was watching me. Not only was he a hundred bucks lighter but he wore (American League President) William Harridge's signature on his leg for a week."

McDermott played for both the Red Sox and the Yankees, but there is no doubt where his allegiance lies. He is a diehard Red Sox fan. "During the 1949 pennant drive we had to win one, and instead we lost two at Yankee Stadium. See, God is a Yankee fan. There was a ball hit to right field and there was a guy named Cliff Mapes playing there. Pesky is on third, and if he scores we win. And I'll be a son of a bitch if a duststorm doesn't come up in right field! In right field! And Pesky can't see the ball to know if Mapes caught it or not. As it cleared, Pesky tagged up, and they tagged him out at home." Ah well, at least He didn't bother hitting us with the plague of locusts.

Mickey McDermott

People who saw Mickey McDermott pitch thought there was no way that the native of Poughkeepsie, NY ("Poughkeepsie is a cemetery with lights," explains McDermott) could miss being a Hall of Famer.

The skinny (170 pounds) 6' 3 " southpaw had blazing speed and a blazing wit. Despite his awesome potential, it is his wit that he is better known for today, and if there were a Hall of Fame for baseball characters, McDermott would be among the first enshrined there.

Bill "Spaceman" Lee after learning of a recent operation undergone by McDermott, quipped: "Mickey McDermott and I are identical twins. The only original body part McDermott has left is his brain." Lee said a mouthful. A more original baseball brain is hard to imagine: Here are some examples of this wondrous organ at work:

"Hitting for me was a gift. I didn't ask for help from Williams or anyone. Ted once took me aside and asked: 'Kid, are you copying me?'"

"The goddamned Yankees were the best hecklers. That goddamn white rabbit, Eddie Lopat, the great left-hander. I was pitching one game and they had a man on first and Lopat was screaming and hollering and raising hell. So I wound up and I made a move to first and threw it right at him in the f—ing dugout. He said, 'You still haven't got control. You missed me by a mile.'"

"I hit a triple once with the Red Sox. I was running like hell and I slid into third and I had been smoking down in the dugout before I came up and I'd put a pack of matches in my back pocket and when I slid they caught fire and there was smoke coming out of my ass and the third baseman said, 'You son of a bitch, you can really run!' The smoke was going like a flamethrower and I was yelling 'Yoww!' I had a f—ing blister on my a— like an apple."

Oscar Melillo

They were on the right track but the wrong train. On July 4, 1937, trains carrying the Boston Red Sox and the Philadelphia Athletics train both left South Station at midnight for games in different cities. In the middle of the night it was discovered that two Red Sox players, Eric McNair and Oscar Melillo were in the right berths, but the wrong train. At first, Athletics players assumed that a secret trade had taken place, and were relieved when the two intruders were let off at Providence.

Lou Merloni

Lou Merloni has lived out the dream of many New England youngsters. Born and still residing in Framingham, Massachusetts, he began his major league career in 1998 with the team he loved as a kid—the Boston Red Sox. Called up to fill in for his pal Nomar Garciaparra, who had suffered a slight right shoulder separation, Merloni flew to Kansas City and arrived around 9:30 or 10 p.m. the night before the game. He realized when he got to the airport that "nobody had told me the name of the team hotel." Should he go to the park? He called Nomar's cellphone, but the evening's game was in progress, and Nomar was in the dugout. After sitting awhile at the airport, and calling from time to time, he finally reached his pal.

He didn't get to the plate in the next three games, but collected his first hit—a single—on May 14. The Red Sox then flew home to host the Royals with Boston mired in a four-game losing streak. Lou's proud parents were in the stands for his Fenway debut, and were also celebrating their 33rd wedding anniversary. Lou's first home appearance came in the second inning, with two men on base. How did the native son handle the pressure of playing in front of friends and family? He homered into the left field screen—a three-run shot off Kansas City Royal pitcher Jose Rosado! The blast provided all the runs the Sox needed, as they beat KC 5-2. One Fenway at-bat, one Fenway homer—instant folk hero.

The *Boston Globe* called it "one of the most electrifying hometown debuts since a 19-year-old kid from Swampscott homered on the first pitch he saw at Fenway in 1964." Conigliaro hit the first pitch; Merloni was working off a 3-2 count. He doubled later in the game and then walked, going 2 for 2.

Lou's second homer was almost an entire season and over 200 at bats later, on October 2, 1999. He was to wait even longer before he'd achieve #3. He didn't hit a single homer in 2000 and it wasn't until September 28, 2001 that he hit his third—it was a pinch-hit ninth-inning home run in Detroit, in a game Boston lost 4-1.

The Monday after that, though, Boston was in Tampa Bay, and Lou hit two more—both in the same game. In one game, he'd equaled his career output between May 15, 1998 and September 27, 2001!

"It was Lou Merloni Night," manager Joe Kerrigan said. "He had a great series [6 for 9 with two home runs, two doubles, and four RBIs]." No, manager Joe Kerrigan did not put Merloni in the cleanup slot the next night. He had his hot-hitting shortstop take the night off.

Dave Morehead

Dave Morehead threw the last no-hitter in Fenway Park. It happened more than a third of a century ago, on September 16, 1965. He'd just turned 23 a few days earlier and was coming off a 1964 season when he was 8-15 with a 4.97 ERA. The game took two hours exactly and boosted Morehead's record to 10-16. No one would have anticipated a no-hitter from the young rightie, especially since he was pitching for a Red Sox team that lost 100 games that year. Only 1,247 fans even bothered to show up at the park that day.

Later that same evening, after Tom Yawkey gave Morehead a thousand dollar bonus, General Manager Pinky Higgins was released and replaced by the capable Dick O'Connell. The move had been planned for some time, and couldn't be deferred despite the awkwardness of announcing it almost literally during the celebration over the no-hitter. It was the third no-hitter for Sox pitchers in four years. Both Earl Wilson and Bill Monbouquette had thrown no-no's in 1962.

Morehead's no-hitter was near the tail end of a lack-luster—well, let's face it, dismal—season for the Red Sox (62-100, 40 games out of first.) His next time out he got bombed, and some wit in the crowd yelled, "Atta boy, Vander Meer!" in mocking reference to the only pitcher to throw back-to-back no-hit games.

One 1966 evening in Lakeland, Florida, Morehead went out with fellow pitcher Earl Wilson and another player to get a drink at a local club called Cloud 9. Seeing Wilson, a black man, the barman said, "We don't serve niggers in herc," so the party got up and left. Sox GM Dick O'Connell told the players to stop going there, but when the Boston press reported the incident, they ignored the bigger story of racial discrimination to chide the trio for going out to drink.

Bobo Newsom

Bobo made more moves than a hobo—and held a job about as long. Bobo played for 17 different teams in 20 years, some of them more than once. The peripatetic pitcher played for the Senators in part of 1935, all of 1936, part of 1937, the beginning of 1942, the end of 1943, the end of 1946 and start of 1947 and lastly, for ten games in 1952. During his travels, he cruised through Boston and won 13 while losing 10 in 1937.

Newsom "kept a hutch of rabbits in his room just for the company. But he forgot about them when he went on the road and they ate their way through the hotel furnishings. Manager Joe Cronin was presented the bill, and soon thereafter Bobo was sent packing." — Okrent & Wulf

You can bet that Jimy Williams would have had him out of there by the fourth inning, but unhampered by any pitch count, Newsom threw 181 pitches and walked ten batters, and *still* managed to win a 1937 game by the score of 3-2.

Russ Nixon

Russ Nixon was traded twice to the Red Sox in 1960. First for Sammy White, then later with Carroll Hardy for Marty Keough and Ted Bowsfield. In 1962, Nixon hit two pinch singles in one inning for the Red Sox.

In a case of premature adjudication, Nixon, catching for the Red Sox against the Yankees, mistakenly thought there were two outs instead of one. When he caught a ball in the dirt on a third strike, he flipped the ball to the batter, Yankee Phil Mikkelson, and trotted back to the dugout. The whole Red Sox team, responding to Nixon's gesture, started to run in as well. Mikkelson tossed the ball into fair territory, towards the mound, and ran all the way around to second before the Sox recovered. Mikkelson later scored.

Trot Nixon

Trot Nixon was the most recent in a lengthy list of players who've started in right field for the Red Sox. The Opening Day right fielder has changed 14 years in a row.

1988	Mike Greenwell
1989	Dwight Evans
1990	Kevin Romine
1991	Tom Brunansky
1992	Phil Plantier
1993	Andre Dawson
1994	Billy Hatcher
1995	Mark Whiten
1996	Rudy Pemberton
1997	Troy O'Leary
1998	Darren Bragg
1999	Trot Nixon
2000	Darren Lewis
2001	Trot Nixon

There have been numerous cases of players being hit in the cup, but usually it doesn't end up as a ground-rule double. On August 8, 2001, with both teams battling for the American League wild-card berth, the Red Sox were playing the Oakland A's in Oakland. In the third inning of that contest, Sox right-fielder Trot Nixon was confronted with a perplexing situation. With Frank Castillo on the mound for the Red Sox in the third inning, Oakland hitter Johnny Damon (now with the Red Sox) lined a shot down the first base line and into the right-field corner. The area was strewn with refuse, and when Nixon went to retrieve the ball he found it firmly lodged in the bottom of a discarded beverage cup. Damon steamed around the bases taking advantage of Nixon's momentary bewilderment. Quickly assessing the situation, Nixon motioned urgently toward the cup, asking for an umpire's ruling. After a long huddle, the umpires ruled it a ground-rule double, despite arguments from Oakland manager Art Howe that it should have been at least a triple.

"I reached into the cup a couple of times and couldn't pull it out," said the right-fielder later. "I gave it a couple of good shakes, and it still wouldn't come out, so I threw the cup with the ball in it into the stands." Where presumably it became a unique souvenir for some lucky fan.

Several months later, Trot told a dinner audience, "Something told me not to mess with it. I did get on TV because of it, though. I wonder how much money we could have made on eBay with that cup!"

Hideo Nomo

Not only did Nomo pitch a no-hitter for the Red Sox in 2001, their first since Matt Young threw one in a losing effort in 1992, but he also was the strikeout king of the American League that year with 220. He had previously won the K crown in the National League in 1995 with the Los Angeles Dodgers.

Buck O'Brien

In 1912, pitcher Buck O'Brien shared accommodations with his catcher Bill Carrigan and Red Sox shortstop Heinie Wagner. One day they were facing the Cleveland Indians and their star, Nap Lajoie. After two quick strikes, O'Brien tried to brush Lajoie back, only to have him pole-ax the ball to the furthest reaches of centerfield and plate two runs. Next time up O'Brien again got two strikes on the Frenchman and then called for a mound conference with his battery-mate.

"What do you want to throw to him?" asked Carrigan. "I think I'll throw an old-fashioned roundhouse curve," came the reply. "I've never tried that on him before. It should catch him by surprise." Lajoie was so surprised that he lashed a bullet straight at Wagner at short. It caught him on the hip and caromed into the outfield. The three roomies gathered at the mound to discuss these events. "Buck," said Wagner, " If you throw that Frenchman any more like that, you'd better find somewhere else to sleep tonight."

O'Brien was 20-13 with a 2.58 ERA for the Sox in 1912, helping them win the pennant. The World Series was rough, though. The Red Sox beat the Giants 4-3 in Game One, then struggled to a 6-6 tie in Game Two, called after 11 innings on account of darkness. Game Three was a 2-1 squeaker, but O'Brien took the loss. Boston won Games 4 and 5, but O'Brien gave up five runs in the first inning of Game Six—and the Red Sox lost, 5-2. O'Brien was 0-2, and it was rumored that he was beaten up by his teammates after the game! The Red Sox denied the reports. The Sox eventually won the Series, but O'Brien—who had been 5-1 in 1911 and won 20 in 1912, sunk to 4-9 in 1913 and was traded to the White Sox later in the year.

Gene Oliver

It was said of weak-throwing former Red Sox catcher Gene Oliver that he had an arm like the Venus de Milo.

Eddie Pellagrini

Like Tony Conigliaro and Lou Merloni, another local who homered in his first Fenway at bat was Eddie Pellagrini. The year was 1946. The date was April 22. Pellagrini recalls that Ted Williams congratulated him, but warned, "Eddie, that's the worst thing you could have done, because now they're going to pitch you like they pitch me!"

Pellagrini had 1,423 major league at-bats, but knocked only 19 others out of parks around the leagues, hitting .226 in his career. His main claim to fame, to hear him tell it, was the year he "led the league in stolen towels."

Johnny Pesky

Johnny "Needle Nose" Pesky set the major league record for the most runs scored in a game, with six on May 8, 1946.

Pesky's 1942 rookie record of 205 hits stood unchallenged until Nomar Garciaparra topped it in 1997 with 209. Pesky totaled over 200 hits each of his first three years in the majors, 1942, 1946 and 1947 (he lost the intervening three years to war.) No one has ever totaled 200 or more hits in each of their first five years in the majors, and Johnny might well have done it for six if the war hadn't intervened.

Johnny was no Ted Williams in the slugging department, however, and never tried to be. Fortunately, Pesky knew his role and played it to perfection, seldom going for the long ball. That didn't stop "Needle Nose" from doing some needling now and again. Johnny wore #6 on his uniform and Ted wore #9. Every so often, Johnny would do a handstand on the field and crow, "Look at me now! I'm Ted Williams!" as his inverted jersey read "9".

Johnny's principal job was to be one of the table setters for slugger Ted Williams and, indeed, in his first six years he scored over 100 runs every year. Johnny was discouraged from trying to stretch a single into a double, nor was he to steal second once on first: in either case, he'd be

Johnny Pesky

leaving first base open with Ted Williams coming to the plate.

Johnny Pesky and Ted Williams are the only two players in ML history to score 100 or more runs in each of their first six years in the majors. Both Earl Combs and Derek Jeter did it six or more consecutive years, but both played a few games the year before their streaks began.

In 1950, Billy Goodman was a super-sub supreme. He had no regular position, and Manager Steve O'Neill moved him around where needed. Goodman clocked considerable playing time in left after Ted Williams broke his elbow in the All-Star Game. The ultimate utility man began to accumulate hits. Late in the season, it became clear that he actually had a shot at the batting title, but with Williams coming back on September 15, and the DH not yet devised, what place was there for Goodman to occupy? The infield was made up of such stalwarts as Walt Dropo (that year's rookie of the year with a .322 average and 34 HRs), Bobby Doerr (.294 average), Vern Stephens (.295 and 30 HRs) and Pesky, who was hitting over .310 at the time. The outfielders were all hitting a ton as well.

Johnny Pesky approached O'Neill and volunteered to yield his position at third base so that Goodman could have a place to play and get the necessary at bats to qualify for the batting crown. O'Neill took him up on the offer, and Billy Goodman earned himself a batting title. It should be no surprise that it was sometimes said Johnny Pesky led the majors in Most Friends.

Jimmy Piersall

Jimmy Piersall's reputation as a flake began with his very first major league at-bat. The nervous rookie outfielder entered the game as a pinch-hitter facing Gene Bearden, the crafty pitcher for the Washington Senators. In his book, Piersall describes the result. (Bearden threw a) "baffling knuckle ball . . . and I was so scared that I threw the bat over the third-base dugout and into the grandstand the first time I ever swung at a ball. Imagine my embarrassment when I found myself standing at the plate without a bat in my hand." Piersall tried to look nonchalant as he strode to the on-deck circle and quietly asked Bill Goodman, "What do I do now?" Goodman gave Piersall a word of encouragement and his bat. Piersall responded by singling to right on a 3 and 2 count.

Piersall's career was interrupted by institutionalization and successful treatment for mental illness. He later commented. "Probably the best thing that ever happened to me was going nuts. Whoever heard of Jimmy Piersall until this happened?"

Asked about the time Piersall sat on second base while Ryne Duren was batting during a game at the Stadium, he said, "Someone said to Casey Stengel, referring to me, 'Is he really Goofy?' Casey said, 'He's the only guy in the park who knows where to play Duren.'"

Jimmy Piersall

Piersall also said, "I was always a Red Sox fan. I hated the Yankees from the day I came out of my mother's womb."

One day Piersall went 6-for-6 at the plate, still tied for the American League nine-inning record, while the great Ted Williams had an off day, going 0-for-4. Piersall could hardly sleep that night, anticipating the glowing reports of his feat in the morning sports pages. "The headline in the paper the next day was that Williams went 0-for-4 for the first time in two years," groans Piersall.

Asked to talk about the time he sat on Babe Ruth's monument in Yankee Stadium, Piersall says: "It was the second game of a doubleheader and we had about eight pitchers walking in and out of the bullpen. So I got tired of that and sat on Babe's monument. I didn't want to make a farce of things, but we were having such a bad day. When the game resumed, the umpire came out and told me I couldn't sit on the monuments. I said to him, 'I'm talking to the Babe.'"

Eddie Popowski

When Eddie Popowski died in 2001, he'd been with the Red Sox for every one of his 64 seasons in pro ball. He'd been a player (stuck behind Bobby Doerr, he never made it to big league play), a coach (1967-74, 1976) and even interim manager of the Red Sox twice — in 1969 and 1973. "The first 50 years were the toughest," he used to say.   Since 1975, he'd been a special assignment instructor along with Johnny Pesky and Charlie Wagner.

Way back in 1931, he'd quit driving an ice truck and taken a job playing with the House of David touring baseball team — and was once stopped by police in Ohio who were searching for John Dillinger. Easy mistake to make: both Dillinger and Popowski were driving Packards. With the House of David, he played against the likes of Babe Ruth and Lou Gehrig, and against Negro League clubs featuring such stars as Josh Gibson and Satchel Paige.

In the 1960s, after Ted Williams had retired, he and Pop were watching a prospect in the batting cage and they differed on his potential. They placed a little one dollar wager, Williams betting the kid would get three hits in that day's game. Instead he struck out three times. Ted tugged a dollar out of his billfold and provided Pop with an instant keepsake: a one dollar bill inscribed, "I lost, Ted Williams." Pop kept that dollar with him until his dying day.

In the fall of 2001, the Red Sox lost Pop, with 64 years of service, switchboard operator Helen Robinson, with 60 years of service and long-time scout Joe Stephenson, who had served the team for 53 years.

Dick Radatz

One of the best relievers of his or any era, Dick Radatz struck out 478 batters in 414 innings over a three-year span.

Even more impressive, over a four-year period from 1962 to 1965, he played a significant role in 149 of Boston's 286 victories! "I was a one-pitch pitcher," said the fireballer from Detroit. "Either hit it or get out. I literally thrived for that one-on-one confrontation. I had to have that challenge like I needed three square meals a day."

Now a radio talk show personality in Boston, the man they called "The Monster" never lost favor with the fans at Fenway. In four-plus years with the Sox, from '62 to the start of the '66 season — some of the most depressingly dismal years in recent Red Sox history — Radatz won 49 and lost 34 for Boston. He was one of the first specialty relievers in the game, often brought in day after day. Twice he led the league in saves, no mean feat for a team that was often in or near the American League basement. More importantly to Boston fans, he was a Yankee killer, mowing down the heavy hitters from the Bronx with apparent ease.

Mickey Mantle had a particularly hard time with The Monster. Mantle faced Radatz 63 times. He managed just one hit — a home run — (yes, that's a .016 average) and struck out 47 times.

Radatz was a mediocre 3-7 in the three years after he left Boston and he credits the atmosphere in Fenway Park for making the difference. "Fenway Park is so intimate it's like playing a slow-pitch game in your neighborhood. And when you're on a roll, the fans are with you. And because I knew the fans were with me, it put a couple of extra inches on the fastball."

Manny Ramirez

Red Sox fans had been all over diminutive Craig Grebeck (5'7", 155 pounds) in 2001 because of his hitting struggles, but the utility infielder quietly played a part in two of the most memorable hits in Fenway Park's recent history.

Frustrated by a string of splintered bats, Manny Ramirez asked Grebeck if he could borrow a few of his bats prior to a Saturday game against Toronto. The results were unforgettable. Ramirez promptly hit a pair of tremendous home runs that together traveled an estimated 964 feet.

On June 23, 2001, Manny Ramirez slugged two home runs at Fenway in a 9-6 loss to the Toronto Blue Jays. Both were powerful blasts. In the first inning, Manny hit a 463-foot homer off the light tower above the fence in left-center field. Ramirez came up again in the third and launched a massive drive high up on the light stanchion behind the Green Monster that fell 12 inches short of glory.

It was estimated as a 501-foot drive, which would make it the second longest in Fenway Park history, trailing only a 502-foot blast by Ted Williams, hit in 1946, and which is memorialized by the famous red seat high up in the right field bleachers.

Many took note of the fact that Manny's home run was judged to have fallen short of matching Ted's record by just one foot. Both were indeed powerful drives, Ted's easily measured, Manny's necessarily estimated. The greater power may well have been that of Red Sox reverence for tradition, and sentiment—when you're an icon like Ted Williams, it's worth at least a foot on the old measuring tape.

Jim Rice

Jim Rice set a major league record by appearing in 163 regular-season games in 1978. Those of you who don't know why there were 163 games in 1978 are suffering from selective amnesia and are no doubt living happy and productive lives wallowing in this blissful ignorance.

From the moment when Ted Williams began playing left field in 1940 (he played 1939 as a right fielder) through Yaz's years and then Rice's which ended in 1987 (as the regular left fielder), just those three Red Sox legends roamed Fenway's left-field grass for 48 years, nearly half a century, save for the years Ted was off at war.

In 1999, many Red Sox fans were outraged when Red Sox ace Pedro Martinez was snubbed for the MVP award in favor of Ivan "Pudge " Rodriguez, the great catcher for the Texas Rangers. Those Red Sox fans with a longer memory, however, were more philosophical, recalling that in 1978 the situation was reversed. Jim Rice captured the '78 MVP title over Yankee pitcher Ron Guidry who won 24 games for the Yankees, lost only three and compiled a microscopic 1.72 ERA. Rice finished the campaign with a .315 batting average and led the league with 213 hits, 46 home runs, and 139 RBIs.

Jim Rice, in *My Greatest Day in Baseball,* gives credits to his teammates: "When you come to my house, my wife's got pictures of Fenway Park, she's got pictures of me sitting on the bench when a guy was doing a photograph session. Everything else in my house—you see books, it's all golf, no baseball. Baseball was more of a team thing. Even the things that I accomplished are because of the team getting me in certain situations. But if you come to my house you'll see all golf books."

Si Rosenthal

Outfielder Si Rosenthal was a Boston native who broke in late in 1925 and enjoyed one solid season with the Sox in '26, hitting .267 with 34 RBIs. A foot injury held him back from a more fruitful major league career, but he did go on to log a .333 average over the next nine years in minor league play. Rosenthal's son Irwin joined the Marines in World War II and was killed in the Pacific on Christmas, 1943. Si himself signed up in the Navy, at age 40. Assigned to the minesweeper *U.S.S. Miantonomah*, Rosenthal was seriously injured in an explosion caused by a German mine off the coast of France and was rendered paraplegic. A few years later, the Red Sox held a "Day" for him and raised money to buy him a specially fitted house.

When Si first signed with the Boston Red Sox organization, Hugh Duffy was the manager. Si told the story like this: "Duffy wanted me to change my name to Rose because it would fit easier in box scores. But I told him that I wouldn't do it. I was born with the name Rosenthal. It won't make any difference if my name is Rose, Rosenthal or

O'Brien. I'll rise and fall on my own name." A rose by any other name. . . .

Pete Runnels

Only five players have ever won two batting titles and still manage to hit under .300 lifetime. A pair of them won two titles for the Red Sox: Pete Runnels (1960 and 1962, lifetime .291) and Yaz (1963, 1967 and 1968, lifetime .285.)

Billy Consolo remembers the battles between Runnels and teammate Ted Williams. "Every time Pete Runnels got a base hit, Ted Williams would just follow him, and Ted had less at bats so he was going up two points when Runnels would go up a point. That's how he won [the batting title]. Runnels hit probably two or three home runs a year. Runnels finally hit a home run and so all of us on the bench said, "OK, now Runnels has got it. I mean, he's *hitting*!" He hit a gut shot out of the ballpark in Washington and Ted Williams followed him with a gut shot over the right field fence. Topped him with every thing he did! If Runnels hit a double, Ted Williams would follow him with a double. It was back and forth. In those days, they didn't have the electronic scoreboard so somebody behind the scoreboard was putting up these numbers. The guy must have been multiplying behind the scoreboard, to the tenth of a point."

Babe Ruth

In 1919, Red Sox pitcher Babe Ruth set the baseball world on its collective ear by poling an unheard-of 29 home runs—more than the rest of the American League combined!

Ruth has had many nicknames in his colorful career, but the one that fit him best was coined in the September 9 issue of the *Boston Post* when they called him "the Prince of Whales" because of "the way you've been whaling the ball all season." He was also referred to as "the mastodon [sic] of hitters, Babe—the dinosaur of slam artists. If you lived in the Stone Age, you'd doubtless be swinging an elm tree at every boulder they pitched to you." Other quotable quotes from that same newspaper account of Babe's exploits include a couple of hyperbolic gems:

"You are the only *20th Century Express* in Baseball, Babe. You never make local stops at second or third. The only place you stop for water is the dugout after you've gone all the way around."

"We'd have a medal struck out for you, but we know you wouldn't care for anything that's been struck out!"

In January of 1920, when Babe Ruth had been sold to the Yankees, the *Boston Post* sub headline was: RUTH TERMED A HANDICAP AND NOT AN ASSET BY THE RED SOX.

What pitcher has the best lifetime record against the New York Yankees? Answer: Babe Ruth, 17-5 for the Red Sox.

On July 11, 1914, pitcher Babe Ruth won his first game for the Red Sox, 4-3. Ruth struck out the first time up and was lifted for a pinch hitter in the seventh. Looking back on Ruth's later successes, can you imagine lifting Babe Ruth for a pinch hitter?

The record for Sox shutouts by a southpaw in a season is 9. It is held by Babe Ruth, a mark he established in 1916. Righties Cy Young and Joe Wood each had 10; Young did it in 1904, Wood in 1912.

Babe Ruth's daughter, Julia Ruth Stevens, threw out the first pitch in Game 4 of the 1999 ALCS vs the Yankees. She was asked why she was cheering for the Red Sox, instead of the Yankees where her famous father had spent most of his career. "Because I think they deserve a break," she said firmly. "Well, they do. They've had a lot of tough breaks. And the umpires certainly haven't made it any easier for them, I must say."   Now that Red Sox ace Pedro Martinez has suggested drilling the Babe in the rear end with a pitch, we wonder if Ms. Stevens' allegiances have been altered.

Gene "Half-Pint" Rye

Gene "Half-Pint" Rye, who for some unknown reason changed his name from his birth name of Eugene Rudolph Mercantelli, came to the Red Sox from Waco in 1931. He arrived with stunning credentials, having hit three home runs in one inning for the Texas team. In the big leagues, the 5'6", 165-lb Rye was not nearly as potent. In 17 major league games he managed seven hits in 39 at-bats for a watered down .179 batting average. Who knows why? Who really cares? The more interesting question is why he changed his name to Rye in the midst of Prohibition.

Ray Scarborough

Ray Scarborough's hometown was Mt. Olive, North Carolina and he spent his winters working as a pickle salesman. No, really—honest to God—he really did.

George Scott

George "Boomer" Scott, Red Sox slugging first baseman, once explained the difference between a streak and a slump: "When you're hitting the ball, it comes at you looking like a grapefruit. When you're not, it looks like a black-eyed pea."

Red Sox manager Dick Williams on George Scott's eating habits: "He looks as though he ate Christmas dinner every night of the week." Williams didn't respect Scott much, and wrote in his autobiography: "Talking to him is like talking to a block of cement."

"It wasn't that George Scott was really that funny," says Bill Lee. "It was just that he came from Greenville, Mississippi, and it's like anyone that comes from Mississippi—you know they're going to rank number 49 or 50 in any category. Boomer was the same. People from Mississippi just thank God that Alabama is down there, too."

Moe Berg's assessment of rookie George Scott in a 1966 interview with a UPI reporter: "I believe there are fortunes to be made by the contractors who replace the walls he will tear down by the force of the baseballs he will hit."

Billy Gardner was known as "Slick" because of his great hands at second base. Mike Barnicle says that while coaching a young George Scott, Slick told Boomer the reason he was so quick was that his father used to "drive golf balls at him from ten yards away and it was either catch the golf ball or die." Whether the gullible George bought that one or not, we can't say.

Reggie Smith

A switch-hitter, on four different occasions Reggie Smith hit homers from both sides of the plate in a game for the Red Sox.

A very powerful player, Smith once picked up Yankee Thad Tillotson during a fight and held him over his head. He then threw him like a medicine ball—and he landed on his feet. Tillotson was listed as a 195 pounder.

Tris Speaker

The Red Sox bought Hall of Fame ballplayer Tris Speaker from the Cleburne, Texas, club for $400. There could have been bidding competition from the Pirates, but Speaker smoked cigarettes, and this didn't sit well with Bucs owner Barney Dreyfuss, who passed on Speaker.

As the Red Sox ace pitcher, Ruth especially admired Speaker for his hitting skills. Ironically, the man who would later become the most feared hitter in the game depended on the Gray Eagle for most of the Red Sox offense. Speaker finished his career with a lofty .344 batting average.

Dave Stapleton

Sox fans are still upset that manager John McNamara did not put Dave Stapleton into Game 6 of the 1986 World Series as a late-inning defensive replacement for Bill Buckner,

Tris Speaker (Brace Photography)

a role he had so often assumed during the regular season. Who can say how that one simple act might have altered Red Sox history?

He may have saved the day (and helped Boston win the World Series) had he been at first base. It would probably have been a routine play and no one would remember it today. Or maybe the ball would have skipped between *his* legs and Stapleton would now be living in seclusion in Idaho instead of Buckner. One thing is certain—his NOT replacing Buckner has made him a rather large footnote in Red Sox history. Fans probably wouldn't otherwise remember Dave Stapleton, even though he did get two hits in three World Series at bats. Ironically, Stapleton is remembered for the play he never got the chance to make.

Stapleton played his entire major league career with the Red Sox (1980-1986), but after that fateful World Series, he never got another chance to play major league ball. An odd quirk, which may explain his early exit from major league competition, is that his batting average declined each and every year of the seven seasons he served the Sox.

1980:	.321
1981:	.285
1982:	.264
1983:	.247
1984:	.231
1985:	.227
1986:	.128

Can any other player boast such a steady, unceasing seven-year decline? Stapleton was clearly going, going, gone. . . . Another couple of years and he could have been the batboy—or even worse, a pitcher.

Jerry Stephenson

Talk about having a bad day! On May 9, 1968, with Jerry Stephenson on the mound for the Red Sox, Ed Stroud of the Senators bunted safely, then stole second. Stephenson balked and Stroud strolled to third. Stephenson finally recorded an out, but then threw a wild pitch and Stroud scored safely. All on a 15-foot bunt.

Dick Stuart

Dick Stuart once hit an inside-the-park homer at Fenway when the ball hit the Wall, then glanced off a fielder's Adam's Apple.

Stuart, who hit 66 HRs one year in the minors, is the only first baseman in ML history to have three assists in one inning. Despite this aberration, he was a klutz in both major leagues. "Dr. Strangeglove" led the league in miscues by first basemen in each of his first seven years, including his rookie year of 1958. That year he played in only 64 games but used the opportunity to commit an impressive 16 first-base errors for the Pittsburgh Pirates. Once he had established his reputation, he built on it throughout his five years in Pittsburgh and then packed his porous glove for the trip to Boston where he topped American League first sackers in errors for two more years.

Dick Stuart (Brace Photography)

The Red Sox first baseman was so bad in the field that it is difficult to exaggerate his level of incompetence. In 1963, he recorded 29 errors at first base, *three times* that of his nearest "rival."

Despite his pathetic fielding, Stuart was an above-average major league hitter. After hitting 35 homers for the National League's Pittsburgh Pirates in 1961, his output fell to just 16 dingers in 1962. Traded to the Red Sox, he assaulted American League pitching for 42 homers in 1963, making him the first player to hit more than 30 homers in each major league.

According to former Red Sox manager Dick Williams, Stuart's clumsiness was matched only by his selfishness. Williams claims that Stuart was once hit by a pitch with the bases loaded and awarded first base by the umpire, scoring a much-needed Red Sox run. Stuart, wanting another chance to hit, denied he was hit, and despite an obvious bruise on his forearm actually succeeded in having the call reversed. Stuart then struck out, ending the Sox rally.

Dick Stuart may have been a one-dimensional player, but that one dimension was power, and he exhibited lots of it in his Red Sox career. Like most power hitters, Stu was always looking for an edge. It is reported that he used to hammer little tacks into the barrel of his bat in order to tighten it up. His teammates were skeptical at best. Carl Yastrzemski laughingly recalls: "If it was a day game and the sun was out, you could see the reflection off the bat from the nails." Even the blindest of umpires couldn't miss that one.

Jim Tabor

Ted Williams' archenemy in the press corps was Dave "The Colonel" Egan, he of the poison pen and nasty disposition, and Ted's battles with Egan were legendary. They were, however, strictly of the verbal and written variety. It took teammate Jim Tabor to actually try to court martial the colonel. While Tabor was in the hospital with appendicitis, Egan had taken a cheap shot at him, suggesting in print that the team was better with him out of the lineup. The bruising and bruised third baseman was in no mood for such jibes. While Tabor was convalescing, he watched the games from the press box at Fenway—which put him in dangerous proximity to his tormentor.

On one famous occasion, Tabor grabbed Egan by the throat and pushed him against the railing beyond which was only an abundance of air and then the screen behind home plate. Before the colonel was thus demoted, General Manager Eddie Collins intervened and saved Egan from a possible fall to earth. There is no truth to the rumor that Ted Williams was on the field, egging Tabor on.

Birdie Tebbetts

Like most catchers, Birdie Tebbetts was notoriously slow of foot on the basepaths. In fact, he was even slow by catchers' standards. They measured his speed to first base with a sundial, and once on first there was little chance of

Birdie Tebbetts (Brace Photography)

advancement other than by a hit. That's why it was some-what incredible that Tebbetts stole five bases during the 1948 season.

One of those five stolen bases came at the expense of Cleveland Indian catcher Jim Hegan, and Hegan was un-derstandably upset by it. "Gene Bearden was pitching," re-called Tebbetts in the *Chicago Daily News*, "and neither he nor Hegan paid any attention to me. I took a pretty good lead and finally lit out. I got to second easy; they didn't even try a play. Somebody doubled and I scored. As I went across the plate Hegan looked at me and said, 'I never came closer to quitting baseball in my life than when you did that.' That's what they think of me on the runways!"

Ted Williams was noted for the intensity of his con-centration. Pitchers and catchers alike would try whatever they could to crack it. Once when he was catching for the Tigers, Birdie tried to do so by telling Ted a long, drawn-out story during an at bat. Ted listened through strike one, and then through strike two. Tebbetts was working up to the punch line when—BAM!—Ted hit the next pitch out of the park. As Ted trotted across the plate, he slowed up briefly. "And then what did she say?" he asked Tebbetts.

Birdie's obituary on the www.thedeadballera.com website reads, in part: "There ought to be a second-string or Junior Hall of Fame for guys like me," he once said. "I had a lifetime average of .270 and I'm proud of it. I poured my life's blood into it. I clawed and scrambled and fought and hustled to get it.

"My whole world is wrapped up in baseball," he said, "and that means I must live the loneliest of lives. I can't discuss my problems with my friends or the newspapermen or the players or the coaches or my wife." His wife, the former Mary Hartnett, understood. One winter night during his days as a manager, the usually talkative Tebbetts was silent as he stared into the glowing fireplace of his home in Nashua, N.H. "What inning are you playing now, dear?" she said.

Luis Tiant

When Luis Tiant went to the Yankees from the Red Sox, he signed on with the Ball Park Franks company as a radio spokesman for their fine hotdogs. It was hard for Red Sox fans to hear El Tiante intone in his best Cuban accent: "It's great to finally be with a wiener!"

In the game of June 14, 1974, Boston at California, Luis Tiant pitched a complete game of 14.1 innings and lost 4-3 on a Denny Doyle RBI double, while Nolan Ryan went 13 innings and struck out 19 while walking 10. Cecil Cooper was 0 for 8 in the contest. Doyle became a Red Sox teammate in 1975. Tiant allowed three runs in the fourth and then pitched 10 scoreless innings until the 15th.

Bill Lee once shared the four-man rotation with Tiant. "Luis Tiant would wind up and throw it, and in the middle of his delivery he'd change it and drop down and throw a slider and do this and that—it was a dance. Luis was just Luis. Every day was a revelation."

Fellow hurler Bill Lee likened a Tiant performance to a concert. "The orchestra comes out and everything starts banging and it shakes the place. Then it comes to the middle part of the symphony and things get very calm and sweet, and you want to kind of fall asleep. Then, all of a sudden, you sense that the end is coming. Everyone starts getting noisy again. The whole gang is letting out with all the instruments. Then, boom! The whole show is over. That's Tiant! Hard at the start, a little sweet, slow stuff in the middle, and then the big explosion at the end." — from Bruce Shalin's *Oddballs*

Shalin himself added, "Luis knew exactly when to turn a bus ride into something out of 'Saturday Night Live.'"

Luis' eccentric rotating windup was perhaps first developed in Cleveland. He called it "The Jaw Breaker."

"My head stops seven times. First I look up; then I look down; then my jaw points toward second base; then toward third. Then it points at the centerfield corner; behind my back; and then — just before I pitch the ball — I point it upstairs near where Mr. Yawkey is sitting."

Dwight Evans on Luis in the 70s: "The one thing that impressed me about those games — and Luis was really the one behind that whole Red Sox era — as soon as he was done warming up and that lever came up from that gate, there was dead silence, and as soon as that latch opened he got a standing ovation all the way to the mound. It was

Luis Tiant (Brace Photography)

exciting for us to see that, and it got us all going, too. It was a tremendous thing." — Bruce Shalin, *Oddballs*

Luis told us: "We used to get Aparicio with rubber snakes. One day I remember we put one in his pants. He ran all the way from the inside out of the clubhouse out all the way to the field! He had his pants hanging down. He's lucky he didn't fall down and get injured."

In 2002, Luis begins work as pitching coach for the Red Sox Single A Lowell Spinners. Now that he's no longer throwing smoke, he's begun to market it. Always known for his trademark cigars, in 2001 Luis launched El Tiante cigars — 23 to a box! Twenty-three was Luis's uniform number with the Red Sox. The wrapper depicts Luis in uniform and the cigars — maduros and rosados — are manufactured by Tabacalera Perdomo in Nicaragua.

"I'd smoke a cigar in the shower, sure. It takes practice. So many years. The water would hit your face and your hair but not hit my cigar. I'd smoke a cigar all the time in the whirlpool."

In the spring of 1988, Luis Tiant pitched for the Red Sox old-timers against the Equitable Old-Timers. He ran into trouble in the first, giving up four runs on a series of bloop hits.

In the dugout between innings, his teammates were waiting for his reaction. He didn't disappoint them. "That was some weak shit," he said, to everyone's amusement. When some players began to rub his arm, Luis quipped: "My arm is fine," he said, turning his rear end to this teammates. "Massage this."

Bob Tillman

In his rookie year, Bob Tillman told a radio reporter, he "couldn't hit a curveball with an oar." Which left him up the proverbial hit creek without a paddle.

Former Red Sox catcher Tillman had a reputation for using the old bean, his own and others. Here are two examples of his heads-up play:

1. With John Wyatt on the mound, a man on first and three balls on the batter, Wyatt pitched to the plate and the runner on first broke for second. The ball was outside—ball four. Wyatt dropped his head in disappointment. However, the catcher, Bob Tillman, caught the ball and pegged a dart toward second base, nailing Wyatt in the side of the head.

2. Needing a baserunner to start a rally, Dick Williams scouted around the dugout for a pinch hitter. Tillman jumped up promising he'd get on base. Williams sent Tillman up to pinch-hit. When the pitch is thrown, Tillman leaned into it, catching it on the side of his helmet-less head and took first on the HBP.

John Valentin

My most embarrassing moment, by John Valentin:

"During spring training of my rookie year, the club went up to Baseball City to play the Royals. I had been told that I would be starting and that the game was to be televised. Oh my, I was so excited. I called my folks, brother, aunts, uncles, cousins, friends, etc. and told everyone that I was playing and to tune in. Just about every television set in northern New Jersey was watching me. I was playing short when a ground ball was hit to me. It was a routine grounder; really a good one that I could handle with ease looking real cool in the process. I fielded the ball and made the toss to first. Since there were two outs I continued after the throw to trot back to the dugout feeling on top of the world. I could just hear Mom say, 'That's my Johnny, atta boy.'

When I got to the dugout, I finally looked up. You see, because I was on TV and a rookie, I was playing it super cool. You know, make the play and trot off the field. Maybe they would even show the play again in slo-mo. The only problem was that there was one out. Not only was I the only player trotting off the field, but the TV camera followed me all the way to the top step. When I reached the dugout, there was nowhere to hide. Turning bright red, I turned around and trotted back to short. The KC crowd gave me a standing ovation. I wanted to replay the last 45 seconds of my life. I wanted to crawl under the turf and hide. Fortunately, no one ever said anything about it . . . not!"

In one 23-month stretch spanning three seasons, John Valentin established himself as perhaps, in the words of Sox fan Steve Mastroyin, the "single most prominent one-game phenomenon player in the history of the Sox." On July 8, 1994 with runners on first and second, the Mariners' Mark Newfield lined sharply to Valentin at short. Val stepped on second, doubling off Mike Blowers, then tagged the oncoming Kevin Mitchell, who was speeding from first base to second. It was only the tenth unassisted triple play in the history of major league baseball. But Valentin wasn't finished.

The following June, Val had a spectacular day at the plate, going 5-for-5 with three home runs. In the process, he became the first shortstop to hit for 15 total bases in one game, and only the eighth Boston Red Sox player to hit three home runs in a game. And there's more.

A year after that, on the 6th of June, 1996, Valentin hit for the cycle in a game against the White Sox. John made his mark in the post-season as well, on October 10, 1999, when he hit two home runs and drove in a total of seven runs, setting a postseason RBI mark.

During the 1999 ALCS, Valentin drove in five RBIs in Game 3 against the hated Yankees. The previous weekend against Cleveland in the Division Series he had hit two home runs in Game 3 and drove in seven in Game 4. As only ballplayers can, teammate Bret Saberhagen gave all the credit to superstition. "We ate dinner at the same place, Saraceno's in the North End," he said. "We sat at the same table. Marie [John's wife] wasn't there last night, but we left her seat open, and I ate the same stuff. If Marie had been there, he wouldn't have been two RBIs short."

Seton Hall Alumni 8, New York Yankees 0. In a May 2, 1995 game between the Yankees and Red Sox, former Seton Hall teammates John Valentin and Mo Vaughn each hit grand slams for the Red Sox, Valentin in one inning and Vaughn the very next inning. The final 8-0 score represented the only time in history that two grand slams had accounted for all the scoring in a major league baseball game. V for Victory!

Valentin had big shoes to fill when he finally made the Red Sox. But ironically he knew the shoes very well thanks to one of baseball's little ironies. "I had an interesting omen occur while I was playing A ball," explains Valentin. "Major League guys often take collections for the minor leaguers. They throw in a box of old spikes, gloves, wristbands, and T-shirts and donate them to the minor league players. A box arrived and the clubby gave me a pair of spikes. They were Luis Rivera's. Two years later when I got called up, I played short replacing Luis Rivera." When Valentin was moved to third base to make room for rookie sensation Nomar Garciaparra, he just had to know! "I asked Nomar if he had received a pair of spikes from me!"

Jason Varitek

Jason Varitek was shortstop on the 1984 U.S. Little League championship team, but by the time he got to Georgia Tech, a skinny kid named Nomar replaced him at short and Tek was sent behind the plate. Varitek thrived at his new position and was chosen to catch for the U.S. Olympic team at the 1992 Barcelona Games. In 1993, he was named *Baseball America*'s College Player of the Year.

Varitek was acquired by the Red Sox along with Derek Lowe for Heathcliff Slocumb and Boston fans still wonder what the Seattle Mariners were thinking when they made the deal. Or indeed if they were thinking at all. On a team

renowned for its bad trades, it was one of the most benefi-
cially lopsided trades in Red Sox history. Slocumb had been
a disastrous 5-15 with Boston—and looked even worse than
his record indicated! He won only seven more games before his career came to a merciful conclusion. Lowe did tremendous work for the Red Sox, including a league-leading
42 saves as a reliever in 2000, before suffering a crisis of
confidence throughout most of the 2001 campaign. Meanwhile Varitek blossomed into one of the league's top offensive and defensive catchers.

With hard work and dedication, Jason Varitek has become Boston's regular catcher and his work ethic and hard-
nosed style reminds some fans of Carlton Fisk. Among his
other talents Jason's training at shortstop earned him the
job of designated catcher whenever knuckleballer Tim
Wakefield took the mound. The "rambling Tek from Georgia Tech" revealed his secret to catching the knuckler: "Pick
it up when it stops rolling."

Mo Vaughn

Ted Williams, who knows something about both hitting and fan abuse, felt some sympathy for Mo Vaughn when
he struggled early in his Boston career. "Mo wasn't welcomed
to Boston with open arms. Despite his superb collegiate
career at Seton Hall, Vaughn heard lots of boos when he
first came up with the Red Sox. I know first hand how tough
Boston fans can be. They take no prisoners and they can
drive you out of town unless you are equally tough. Once
they are in your corner, however, they are the most loyal
fans in the world."

Mo was a fan favorite in Boston, though he seemed to wear out his welcome with some fans. Red Sox management seemed not to want him, and Mo got the message—though he was hurt and wore it on his sleeve a little. Those who reviled him pointed out how he'd become an habitue of a "gentleman's club" called the Foxy Lady. One night he overturned his car while returning home from the club at 2 a.m. Red Sox fans got on his case as only they can do, calling him "Mo' Money" after he signed for $80 million with the California Angels despite telling a Boston sports talk radio show, "It isn't about the money."

Harking back to Clemens' ride on police horse Timothy in 1986, when the Sox clinched a spot in the playoffs in 1995, Mo Vaughn was talked into riding a Boston Police horse. "I'll never ride a horse again," Vaughn later vowed. "Everybody was saying, 'You gotta ride the horse, you gotta ride the horse. The horse is good luck.' The horse is not good luck—I was zero for 14 in the playoffs." Red Sox CEO John Harrington, asked about concern his star ballplayer could have been hurt, joked, "I was worried about the horse."

Charlie Wagner

Charlie Wagner was thrown out of only one game during his years in the majors and it was just for trying to get a little summer tan.

Wagner had pitched the day before and was in the visitors clubhouse in Detroit, so he missed umpire Bill Summers ordering Tom "Scoops" Carey off the top step of the dugout. In the early 1940s players were not supposed to sit on the top step of the dugouts at Briggs Stadium. Summers and Jimmie Foxx had been going at it a bit, but things had calmed down when Wagner emerged and sat down there to catch a few rays. Next thing he knew Summers was coming over, barking at him, "All right, Broadway. You're out! Get going!"

Wagner awoke as out of a trance, Roger Birtwell reported in the *Boston Globe*, and asked, "Eh-what? What's that, Bill? I didn't say anything. What did I do?"

"Never mind," roared Summers, "Get out of the park." So Wagner ended up with a Summers ban instead of a summer tan.

Murray Wall

When folks talk about "The Wall" in Fenway, it's a safe bet that few are thinking of Murray. This Wall started with the Boston Braves in 1950, appearing in one game in early July and working four innings. He gave up six hits and had five runs scored on him, and then disappeared from major league rosters for several years.

Wall never gave up, however, and in 1957 he was back with Boston, this time with the American League's Red Sox. He went 3-0 that year, and followed up with an 8-9 record and respectable 3.62 ERA in 1958. Homers hit off him over the Green Monster were said to have been "Wall to Wall" homers.

The next year Wall was 1-4 with a 5.40 ERA when he was abruptly traded to Washington for Dick Hyde, who turned out to be something of a Dr. Jekyll. It seems that Hyde had hidden a sore arm and the trade was rescinded, but not before Wall had pitched one and one-third innings for the Senators, giving up a home run and two other hits. Hyde returned to the Senators and Wall wended his way back to Boston, having recorded the shortest and most unproductive stay in Washington since President William Henry Harrison.

Wally "The Green Monster"

When Wally made his first public appearance on April 13, 1997, he was booed lustily by some elements in the crowd—just as a few other left-field denizens at Fenway have been. Wally's initial introduction to Fenway Park was even the subject of a question in the April 14, 1997 Department of State briefing by spokesman (and Red Sox fan) Nicholas Burns. Mr. Burns was not pleased about the emergence of a mascot at Fenway Park. From the official record, Burns is quoted: "I think it's an abomination. Don't you? It's an abomination. It's an affront to our decent values and right thinking. Do you know what we're talking about? This new mascot, Wally the Green Monster at Fenway Park." Burns later was sent to Greece to serve as United States Ambassador to that faraway land.

Wally turned out to be a humanitarian of the first order, though, and his good works won over even his most vocal critics. Today Wally does a great deal of charity work in the Greater Boston area, particularly with children in need. He bears a resemblance to Oscar the Grouch although his disposition is much brighter and his hygiene impeccable. As with many celebrities, his popularity soared following a number of appearances on television, in Wally's case aided by the invaluable PR he received from cronies Jerry Remy and Sean McDonough on Red Sox telecasts.

Wally became so popular that in September 1999, he was rewarded by being taken on a road trip. It turned out to be an eventful one for the little guy. On September 5 in Seattle, early in the West Coast swing, Wally was struck by a foul ball off the bat of Nomar Garciaparra as horrified viewers back home watched the Sunday game on live TV. The blow knocked him off his perch atop the TV monitor and he had to be taken from the broadcast booth on a tiny stretcher hastily fashioned out of Popsicle sticks. A tiny ice pack (one cube in a little sack) was placed on his head. He reported that everything was a bit fuzzy until he realized that he was looking at his own nose. Nomar was as upset as anyone in the ballpark. Wally was attended to by team doctors and then taken to a nearby hospital for an MRI, which proved negative.

A few days later, Wally was fully recovered and—apparently feeling his oats a bit on this first trip away from Fenway—went out on the town with Rich Garces and Pedro Martinez and stayed out a little too late. Wally was grounded for breaking curfew; the pitchers reportedly got off easier. Jerry Remy explained, "Wally is still learning how to travel. He hasn't traveled much, you know." Wally settled down and stayed pretty low-key until he got back to Boston.

Wally did get a little boisterous at the Ryder Cup and was actually detained by security personnel at The Country Club, and arrested for heckling.

Wally "The Green Monster" (The Boston Red Sox)

"He knows very little about golf etiquette," commented Jerry Remy afterwards, again excusing Wally's inappropriate behavior. Bewildered a bit by the intoxication of his sudden rise to fame, and perhaps a little chastened, Wally snapped to again and settled back into a baseball groove. On his first visit to New York, he visited Monument Park inside Yankee Stadium where, showing courage and pluck of the first magnitude, he stared down the Babe himself, an act that won him even more admirers back home as the Sox swept that series. His showdown with the Babe is also said to have inspired Pedro Martinez to make an even more blatant challenge to the Bambino (See Martinez entry for details).

Perhaps recalling Clinton appointee Nicholas Burns's slur on his character, it is hardly surprising that Wally decided to throw his Red Sox hat into the ring in the 2000 federal election. He announced his candidacy for the President of the United States, carrying the banner of the newly formed Mascot Party. Unfortunately his life came under the media microscope and rumors of scandal plagued his campaign. He was seen talking on his cellphone to female fans in the stands during Sox games. That was just the beginning. The name "Slick Wally" started to appear on internet sites as unsubstantiated accusations of a romantic involvement with tennis glamour girl Anna Kournikova spread. This scandal-mongering backfired however, and his "friendship" with Kournikova made him even more popular than ever.

Just as this scandal began to subside, reports circulated about a brawl with former Yankee player Bucky Dent. Again, these reports only served to increase his popularity with Boston voters, although presumably not in voter-rich New York. Wally had no shortage of potential running mates, and the media buzz suggested that the fuzzy thinkers such as the Philly Phanatic, Pat Patriot and Ross Perot were on his short list.

Wally stayed quiet throughout 2001, a generally uninspiring year for all Sox fans. Wally huddled with potential buyers for the Red Sox but wisely declined to join any particular group. As we go to press, though, there are rampant rumors about Wally's seething ambition to replace Sean McDonough as Jerry Remy's broadcast partner. Wally will be 90 in 2002, but that never held back Strom Thurmond. It's possible that he may mount a bid for a U.S. Senate seat if John Kerry runs for President. Bosox fans everywhere hope the little guy gets to see the Red Sox win another World Championship before too long. He's been waiting since 1918.

Earl Webb

His career may have been short—a mere 650 games—but while in the major leagues, Earl Webb tried to double his fun. He totaled 155 lifetime two-baggers, and in 1931 banged out 67 for the Red Sox, a major league record. The previous year he had 30, and in a 1932 season split between Boston and Detroit, managed another 28. The closest any player has come to Webb's mark in the last 70 years is Todd Helton's 59 in 2000.

Billy Werber

Baseball humor exists at all levels. Billy Werber was a practical joker and a Duke graduate. "He was never without a firecracker, an electric buzzer to shake hands with, a stink bomb or any other weapon of that kind on which he could lay his hands," wrote one Werber observer. Among the stunts he pulled were putting a possum in Johnny Orlando's hotel bathroom, a stink bomb in Tom Yawkey's bedroom on the train and a dead fish in Al Schacht's berth. He gave Dolf Luque a mutilated necktie into which he'd sewn bolts, screws and buttons. All that was missing from Werber's repertoire was the fake dog doo-doo.

When the reconstructed Fenway reopened in 1934 and the players showed up to see their new clubhouse in April, they found that "the floor was covered with a thick layer of wood dust, and several area alley cats, none of which had signed a Red Sox contract, were in obvious residence." One of the players gave a broom to outfielder Dusty Cooke. Bill Werber said, "A cat would jump on top of a locker and run its length with Dusty swinging wildly and overcoat flying. The dust was so thick in the air, he looked exactly like Lawrence of Arabia in a sandstorm. The cats escaped through an open transom, leaving behind cheering Red Sox, atop stools, sore from laughing and covered with dust."

Billy Werber was a swift and aggressive baserunner. On August 24, 1934, Werber was walked in a game against the Tigers. As he trotted down toward first, he noticed that neither the shortstop nor second baseman was paying attention. So he turned on speed as he hit the first base bag and made it safely to second before either infielder could get into position to take a throw. The catcher indeed threw wildly into center, and Werber wound up at third. He scored the tying run on a sac fly.

On opening day 1935, Yankees catcher Bill Dickey dropped a third strike, then fired the ball to first. An alert Werber, who had been on third base, saw his opportunity, shot home and scored the winning run in a 1-0 Red Sox victory.

Werber told us, "I remember a lot of jokes I did play. I don't mind sharing one of them that was very effective. Wesley Ferrell was a single fellow and he rented Chevrolet cars when he was in Spring training in Florida.

"The Chevrolet car sat out in front of the Sarasota Terrace Hotel. It was sitting out there one evening after dinner, and I went out behind the hotel and I got a double handful of crab guts and fish heads and stuff like that and I went to his car and I put all of that junk behind the seat. Not under the seat in the rear, but behind it. I took the seat out and I put it behind there. There it sat all the next day, in the hot sun. Roy Johnson asked Wesley if he could borrow the car that night. He had a date and Wesley wasn't going to use it and he said sure and gave him the keys.

"Well, when Roy Johnson opened the door, it like to knocked him down. That smell. There was a pair of pants and a pair of shoes lying on the floor there in the back and Roy threw those out on the grass. Wesley fished in Lake Myaka.

"Roy went on down to pick up his date and when they came back by the hotel they had all the doors open. Roy was out one side and the girl was out the other. Somebody asked him the next day how things went.

"'Not too good,' he said. 'She thought it was me and I thought it was her.'

"Now the next day, Wesley pulled the stool out of his locker and said if the no-good S.O.B. would acknowledge that, he'd whup him! And if two guys had anything to do with it, he'd whup 'em both. All the players were sitting around laughing and clapping and shouting 'Give it to him, Wesley! Give it to him, Wesley!' He never did find out who did that.

"He was so mad. He couldn't use his Chevrolet after that. He had to turn it in."

Tom Werner

One of the new Red Sox owners, Tom Werner, had an early Fenway connection. Though born in Manhattan, Werner recalls becoming entranced with Fenway early on. "I remember going to Red Sox games when I went to Harvard over 30 years ago," Werner said. "I would take off a lot of time and ditch classes, and come to Fenway Park in the afternoon."

In 1971, the Harvard senior produced a short documentary film about Fenway Park — and later went on to produce "The Cosby Show," "Roseanne," "3rd Rock from the Sun" and other popular TV shows.

Sammy White

"OK, catcher. I've seen enough. You just don't have it today. Hit the showers!" When Boston pitcher Bill Werle missed the strike zone with nine consecutive pitches during a game in 1954, manager Boudreau came out and pulled catcher White, not pitcher Werle.

Del Wilber

This Sox catcher pinch hit in '53 and drove a home run off the first pitch thrown to him. Next time up, same thing. Two pitches, two pinch-hit homers.

Jimy Williams

During Jimy Williams's tenure as Red Sox manager, he compiled an enviable 414-352 win-loss record (.541 winning percentage) and although his on-field strategies sometimes baffled Sox fans, his baseball know-how won admirers throughout baseball. He was voted manager of the year in the A.L. in 1999 and at the time of his abrupt dismissal in the midst of the 2001 pennant race, he had the injury-ravaged Red Sox 12 games over .500 with a 65-53 record, just two games out in the wild-card race and not far behind the league-leading Yankees. The team collapsed after his departure, playing sub .500 ball the rest of the way.

Bill Lee: "Jimy Williams did a great job of pissing everybody off and getting them to do things they never would have. Jim Palmer was like that with Earl Weaver.

"Dick Williams was like that in 1967 when we won the pennant."

Williams was criticized for being less than open with the media and fans. He often refused to discuss strategic moves, cutting off reporters' questions with the blunt explanation "manager's decision."   Some of his homegrown expressions rivaled Yogi Berra for their obscurity.

Some examples of what the *Boston Globe* termed "Jimywocky":

During his first press conference as Red Sox manager in 1996, Williams stunned the Boston media with the following observation: "If a frog had wings, he wouldn't bump his booty."

Williams was once asked about a home run by Manny Ramirez that appeared to start out foul and then turn fair: "I'm not the ball. I think the ball is the only one who knows."

Asked to assess Japanese reliever Tomo Ohka's fastball, he said: "He had some giddy-up. How do you say giddy-up in Japanese? 'Hi-ho, Silver?'"

When asked if reporters could see him earlier in the morning, he replied: "As long as I've got my cup on."

When he was asked under what conditions his base runners should steal, he offered the following thoughts: "The runner dictates it. The pitcher dictates it. The catcher dictates it. The score dictates it. The situation dictates it. But I'm not a dictator, whatever that means."

His reaction to Seattle's Kingdome being torn down: "One less racquetball court."

Asked to pinpoint his hometown of Arroyo Grande, California: "It's about three miles past 'Resume Speed.'"

Fall 2001, with Sox pitching in shambles, everyone wondered who'd be starting when the team returned from Cleveland. Williams was asked about the state of his rotation. His response? "It's in Ohio, and Friday it will be in Boston."

When asked if the '99 Sox were a surprise, Williams answered, "I don't know about that, surprise, or all those other adjectives, or what do you use, adverbs? Prepositions? I like gerunds. I went to high school with a guy named Gerand Thornquist. His dad drove a bus for Greyhound. He was almost the valedictorian. You'd have to be with a name like that."

No one can remember the question, and it became irrelevant when Williams responded, "I guess, you know, when I was a little kid, I liked to play marbles. You know, everybody has different games they like to play. I liked to play marbles. A lot of you people think I've lost mine, I don't know. I still got them at home in a big brandy snifter. I really do."

Williams is highly regarded in baseball and was quickly snapped by the Houston Astros practically the minute the season was over. One assumes he will adapt to his new environment. Jimy was once asked to offer his evaluation of Enron Field (which happened to be the home of the Astros before they bought back the naming rights in the wake of the Enron scandal): "What position does he play?"

Ted Williams

Ted Williams was truly in another league when it came to hitting. Williams batted a cool .344 in a career that began in 1939 and ended with a dramatic homer in 1960 (with interruptions for service in WWII and Korea.) During that same period, the American League average was .260, a 0.84 differential.

Fans in New York and Boston still argue about which is the more incredible baseball feat: Joe DiMaggio's 56-game hitting streak, or Ted Williams's .406 batting average. Both took place in 1941. There is no question that Ted had the better offensive numbers for that season. He hit 37 homers to Joe's 30; his on-base percentage of .551 bested Joe's .440 mark; his slugging average was .735 to Joe's .643, and of course he out-hit DiMaggio .406 to .357. But how did the two men compare during the 56-game streak? Joe batted a stellar .409 during his streak, but that was only a mere three points higher than the average that Ted maintained over the course of a full season.

Hank Aaron: "I'd have to agree that 56, 755, and .406 are three of the most significant numbers in baseball history. When fans think about hitting streaks, they think DiMaggio; when they think about home runs, it's me or Ruth. But when you think about hitting, it's Ted Williams and .406."

In 1942, Ted Williams won the Triple Crown with a .356 batting average, 36 homers, and 137 RBIs. Ted also led the A.L. in runs, bases on balls, total bases, slugging percentage and on-base percentage, as well as in runs produced. The Yankees' Joe Gordon batted .322, hit 18 homers, and drove in 103 runs. What did Gordon lead in? Only two statistics—strikeouts (with 95) and grounding into double plays. He also committed 28 errors, more than any other player at his position. So who was voted American League MVP in 1942? Joe Gordon by a vote of 270-249.

In Korea, Ted served his second tour of duty (he'd already given up three years of his career to serve in World War II), this time as a United States Marine fighter bomber pilot. He served in the same squadron as John Glenn, and was Glenn's wingman on many missions. Twice Ted's plane was hit by enemy ground fire, and once his jet exploded in flame just seconds after he crash-landed it on a nearby base. Glenn offered an appraisal of Ted's contribution:

"I'd guess probably half the missions that Ted flew in Korea he flew as my wing man. . . . He did a great job and he was a good pilot. He was out there to do a job and he did a helluva good job. Ted ONLY batted .406 for the Red Sox. He batted a thousand for the Marine Corps and the United States."

Ted Williams never got beaned in the majors, but he did get hit in the head once in the minor leagues. "Bill Zuber got me in the back of the head," recalls Ted. Sid Hudson came closest to beaning Ted in the majors. "I went to a 3-2 count on him in Washington and he hit the bill of my cap and turned my cap right around."

Billy Consolo recalls: "Ted Williams. 1953. I was in the clubhouse when he was coming back. I saw them put this uniform in the locker. Number 9. I said, 'Oh, my God.' My locker was right near the toilet. Of course, all the rookies get right near the toilet, you see. I was six lockers down from him. He had two lockers. Everybody else had one. He was next to the bat rack also. Johnny Orlando put out that uniform and, boy, I sat in my locker until he walked in—with about a hundred sportswriters. And cameras. Those old cameras. These were those tripod things. And they were shooting him. I mean to tell you, I get chills even talking about that day.

"Then he went out and took batting practice. With his golf gloves. Nobody used golf gloves in those days. They call them batting gloves now. He had been out of shape. They gave him about 30 days to get in shape so he wore those gloves to protect his hands. He had to start off from scratch. That was exciting. That was quite a day.

"And then to see him come out of the ballpark at night after a ballgame, and those people just a hundred deep. They wouldn't let his car out of the parking lot. They wanted to see him, touch him. He never traveled with us in the end. He and Paul Schreiber—the batting practice pitcher—they roomed together at different hotels than where we stayed. He couldn't walk through the lobby of a hotel, with people knowing the Red Sox were in that hotel. It was like playing with Babe Ruth."

The Splendid Splinter carried on a tempestuous feud with the Boston press, giving them the finger, spitting at the press box, making remarks about the smell of manure as he'd pass a reporter in the clubhouse. His boyish Western enthusiasm was met with some cynicism by a hard-drinking press corps who seemed to resent the too-good-to-be-true youngster from the Coast. When they starting prying into his family, Ted felt they'd crossed the line in the competitive quest for headlines, using him—even prodding him —for fodder, and he withdrew. As time went on, he learned to work the press, and there are those that allege he stirred up some of the controversy himself later on as a way to energize himself, to pull himself out of slumps. He often seemed to explode out of a doldrums after one of the incidents.

"I put up with a lot of nonsense from Ted. I started covering baseball in '51 or '52. It was tough in the press box, especially when you're breaking in new. I was fresh out of college, and I ran into a buzz saw with this guy. I was kind of proud, got a job with a metropolitan newspaper, and all of a sudden this guy's telling me I'm a bum. He was tough. He was indiscriminate." —Tim Horgan, *Boston Herald*

"The fans turned on him. I think because he is a combative person that it actually fed him and he used it. Some shrinking violets would have been crushed by that sort of treatment, but he was a courageous, stand-up guy and that fed him. He likes competition, he likes rivalry, he likes an argument. He had a different personality from DiMaggio and Musial who were both quiet guys who kept to themselves and weren't flamboyant." —Paul Gleason, actor and friend of Ted Williams

"What made Ted great was that he refused to think that a pitcher could get him out. I mean he just refused to buckle, and that's what it takes to be great. Somehow you've just got to feel that you are the best. That's how he played

the game and that's how he left the game, as the best"—
Hank Aaron

Billy Consolo adds another memory: "When I was a kid 18 years old, I remember going north, barnstorming, with Ted Williams, and every town we went into—like Bloomfield, South Carolina, towns like that—the whole town would show up to see one man: Ted Williams. They didn't even know who the other players on the Red Sox were. It was only one guy. There were people sitting on mountains, looking over ballparks in the south. One game every day. You'd get on the train and barnstorm north. We used to go up with the Phillies a lot of times and the Braves a lot of times. But everybody came to see Ted Williams, let's face it. It was jam city when he played. That was exciting."

Ted loved to fish in New Brunswick, Canada, and keeps a house there on the Miramichi, one of the world's great salmon rivers. He's also helped inspire the battle to save the endangered Atlantic salmon and he still funds the Ted Williams Conservation Award, a highly prized award for writers who have helped the cause. In 2001, Ted was inducted into the Atlantic Salmon Hall of Fame and author Jim Prime accepted on Ted's behalf.

Those who know sport fishing considered Ted one of the greatest sport fishermen of all time. He's a member of the International Game Fish Association Hall of Fame and still holds the record for one of the largest fish ever caught (off the coast of Peru.) Ted's fishing prowess has been reflected in his induction into two other halls of fame for anglers: the Atlantic Salmon Hall of Fame and the National Freshwater Fishing Hall of Fame.

In all, Ted Williams is a member of the following Halls of Fame:

San Diego Hall of Champions
National Baseball Hall of Fame
Atlantic Salmon Hall of Fame
National Freshwater Fishing Hall of Fame
International Game Fish Association Hall of Fame
Boston Red Sox Hall of Fame
United States Marine Corps Sports Hall of Fame
Florida Sports Hall of Fame
Hispanic Heritage Baseball Museum

One Hall of Fame that has not inducted Ted is the Hitters Hall of Fame in Hernando, Florida—but that is because it is part of the Ted Williams Museum and Ted specifically asked that he not be included.

The Ted Williams Museum is the first museum ever dedicated to a living athlete. Visitors can view taped video tributes to Ted recorded by four United States Presidents—Richard Nixon, Gerald Ford, Ronald Reagan and George H. W. Bush.

Ted is closest to George Bush, a former college first baseman at Yale, and President Bush participated in the Museum's annual event in 1995. Ted has campaigned for a number of political candidates for office—so long as they're Republican.

Ted's father was a friend of California's Governor Merriam. When the young Ted was first introduced to Merriam, with typical unselfconscious irreverence, he simply greeted the Governor with a spirited "Hiya, Guv!"

> *"I just wish I could have voted for you. But you had to be a $%#@% Democrat!"*
> —Ted Williams to astronaut and former US Senator John Glenn at "An Evening with #9 and Friends" in 1988.

I hardly know Ted. The only time I remember Ted was when we played him in the All-Star Game in Fenway Park, in 1946. He hit a couple of home runs and I was playing shortstop, and as he rounded second base he looked over at me and gave me a big wink, and he says, "Kid, don't you wish you could hit like that?"— Marty Marion

Vic Power remembers an episode from his past that is reminiscent of Tom Sawyer's famous whitewashing encounter. "I played with some characters. Like Tony Oliva. . . . Well, I was living in Minnesota. It's cold up there during the winter and I had to get up every morning to shovel snow to take my car out of the garage to drive my kids to school. I was tired of it.

"I was reading in a psychology book that in life man takes advantage of other men to get ahead. Okay, I thought, let me see if this works.

"Now I'm sitting in my house with Tony. I said, 'Tony, you know what I just read? I was reading Ted Williams's book, and Ted said that the secret to his success was shoveling snow.'

"Ted Williams was the greatest hitter—the most power, the most intelligent, the last guy to hit .400. And he said his secret is shoveling snow."

"The next day Tony was at my house with a shovel. I was inside laughing, and he was outside shoveling snow. Then come October, the end of the season, and Tony Oliva was the batting champion. He said, 'Vic, you were right.'

"And now look what happened: Kirby Puckett became the batting champion. I think he's been telling Puckett to shovel snow."   —*They Played the Game*

The following story from *A Bittersweet Journey* explains a lot about the drive that made Ted Williams the greatest hitter of them all. Jimmy Piersall recalled,

"They were tough on him, but you know why? They sort of sensed that when they got on him, he played better. He hit better. Ted used to say to me when I got mad about something, 'I'll take care of it, kid. Don't worry.' He used to talk through his teeth when he got mad. I said, 'Ted, why are you getting so mad all the time?' And he said, 'You know why? Because I've got to be good every day. You don't.'"

Ted, on not wanting to settle for a .3995 on the last day of the 1941 season: "I want to have more than my toenails on the line." Ted chose to hit, and went 6-for-8, boosting his average to .406.

How often does a ballplayer demand a decrease in salary? Ted did, after he only hit .254 in 272 at-bats in 1959.

"I'd just go in and see Mr. Yawkey, and we'd talk a little fishing and we'd talk a little hunting, and he'd ask me how I felt, and I'd sit down and sign my contract. They doubled my salary every year for the first five years, and when it got to $125,000, they kept it there every year for the last ten years. But when they gave me the usual $125,000 for the 1960 season, I tore it up right in Mr. Yawkey's face. I threw it down on the table and told him to give me $90,000, because that's all I deserved."

Actor Paul Gleason, who was friendly with beat generation writer Jack Kerouac, reports that the young Kerouac admired Ted's rebel side and would often hitchhike into Boston from his native Lowell to catch games in Ted's first few years. "He let things flow and that was what Kerouac looked for in everything in life—people who didn't revise their behavior, didn't conform . . . in Ted's case, he just let it fly."

"Ted the first rebel? No. A rebel to me is a guy who goes out of his way to create problems. Ted was absolutely true to himself. I don't think there was anything rebellious about it. I think the guy was just honest, the first really honest guy. And maybe the last one, too."—Bobby Knight

Ted's high school principal Floyd Johnson appreciated his attitude.

"When Williams attended Hoover High School, he habitually dropped into my office for a chat. During these chats, it never occurred to me that Ted would usually slump down into his chair and put his feet up on the principal's desk. The subject would usually be either baseball or fishing, subjects I was just as interested in as Ted. And I'd be enjoying the conversation so much I'd be completely oblivious to his posture and unconventional way of talking to the school principal. This was never impudence on Ted's part. To him all folks on the school campus were the same— faculty, principal, or kids." —*Ted Williams* by Arthur Sampson

Sparky Anderson wrote:
"In spring training a while back, we played the Red Sox in Winter Haven.

"In batting practice before the game, a man walked up to shake my hand.

"'Hi, Sparky. I'm Ted Williams,' he said.

"I almost fell over. I started to laugh.

"'Ted, that's the funniest thing I ever heard,' I said.

"'What do you mean?' he said.

"'You telling me that you're Ted Williams,' I answered. 'Everybody knows you. You don't have to say who you are.'

"'No, Sparky, it can't be that way,' he explained. 'I would never want you to be embarrassed if you happened to forget who I was.'

"Now just imagine. This was Ted Williams. This was one of the greatest players in the history of our game making sure that I wasn't embarrassed.

"That's not only success. That's class.

"After that, I never meet anyone to whom I don't introduce myself before the other guy gets a chance. I always walk up with my hand out. 'Hi, I'm Sparky Anderson.'"

—*Sparky!* by Sparky Anderson

Talk to players from the 1950s. Every one of them will tell you: when Ted stepped into the box to take batting practice, everyone else stopped and watched. Then silence was punctuated only by the hard shots of balls hit deep. "It was a picture swing," says former roommate Broadway Charlie Wagner. "You don't have to be prejudiced about it. He stopped everything in the ballpark, just with his swing. When he went to bat in batting practice, the whole park got silent as a church. Beautiful swing. A classic swing. Nobody's had it since."

When Ted took over right field for the Red Sox in 1939, he displaced Ben Chapman, who had hit .340 the year before. It wasn't all bad news for Chapman. Forever afterward, harking back to an earlier job change, he bragged that he lost his job twice to two good men — to Joe DiMaggio of the Yankees and Ted Williams of the Red Sox.

In his book *Oddballs*, author Bruce Shalin talks about becoming a navel explorer courtesy of Ted Williams.

"Both leagues had just made an adjustment in the strike zone for the '88 season, so I asked Williams what he thought about it. 'Where's my belly button?' he growled. I pointed at his midsection, and he said, 'Where is it? Show me where it is!' I pointed my finger at his waistband. 'No, that's not it!' He pulled down the waistband of his baseball pants, grabbed my finger and stuck it in his belly-button. So there I was, with my finger in the navel of the greatest hitter who ever lived. 'Here it is,' he said. 'Now this ball at the belly-button has got to be a strike.'"

Ted invited Tony Gwynn to receive an award at the Ted Williams Museum's annual event in 1995. Tony doesn't like dinners and awards, but this was, of course, Ted Williams making the invitation. Tony told his agent John Boggs, "There'll probably be a million people there and I'm going to get some award and probably see Ted Williams for about two seconds."

That was basically what happened the first evening. The next day, it looked like a reprise of the evening before when Bob Costas asked Tony to sit down for a one-on-one discussion between him and Ted. "We went back there," Boggs recalls, "and it was Costas and his producer, the cameraman, technician, President Bush, Ted Williams and Tony. And I'm sitting there thinking, 'Man, this is unbelievable.' President Bush left and Tony took the President's seat, and they started talking. And I am telling you, it was like the student and the pupil. You could tell that Tony wanted to relate his batting theories when Ted was asking the questions, but always had this hesitancy he was going to say the wrong thing. You got this sense of relief every time Ted would say, 'Absolutely!'"

Tony himself adds, "I was like a kid in a candy store. When he was talking, I was like a little kid. But I hung in there and made a few of my points, talked about how I do it. That was clutch."

A Red Sox utility player had just returned from a public appearance for which he was paid the grand sum of $35. He met Ted Williams who was on his way to another appearance—this one for $1,000. "How can they justify the difference in money?" whined the long-forgotten player. "Just think of it as the difference between .238 and .388," explained Ted.

Having tried unsuccessfully to get Ted out any other way, former teammate Jimmy Piersall came up with a unique new strategy to foil the Splendid Splinter. With Ted at the plate in the late innings of a close game, Piersall, now playing outfield for the Cleveland Indians, sprinted back and forth repeatedly from his position in center field to left field. Instead of distracting Ted, the bizarre maneuver got Piersall ejected from the game.

Ted Williams was asked if the inside-the-park homer he hit to win the pennant-clinching game in 1946 was the easiest he ever hit. "Hell no, it was the hardest. I had to run."

What about the Holy Ghost? Ted Williams hit a HR off Thornton Lee in his first year, 1939 (the 28th of his career) and off Thornton's son Don Lee (the 517th) in September, 1960, the final month of his final year.

In 1999, Ted Williams was back in Fenway Park for the third, and possibly last All-Star Game ever to be played there. Once again, he was the center of attention as current stars and Hall of Famers gathered around him, like starry-eyed kids. True to form, Ted could be heard giving hitting instruction to Mark McGwire and Sammy Sosa, who had only combined for 136 homers the previous year.

Ted claims that he can remember in detail each of his first 300 major league home runs—who the pitcher was, what the count was, the kind of pitch and where the ball landed. He also remembers the strikeouts. Billy Crystal, a great Yankee fan, once cornered Ted Williams at a card-signing show and informed him that he had home movies of Ted striking out. The actor-comedian related a specific time more than three decades previous, when Ted had struck out in a key situation against a Yankee pitcher. Ted nodded knowingly. "Curveball," he said. "Low and away."

Ted managed the Washington Senators in 1969. The team performed well above expectations, as did several individual players. Ted was voted Manager of the Year, but he was on safari in Africa when the award was announced. Told he'd been honored as Manager of the Year, Williams expressed pleasure but then added, "I'll tell you something. It was just another case of the writers being wrong again. Weaver and Martin deserved it more."

Umpire Joe Paparella told Larry Gerlach about Ted's uncommon courtesy. "I worked with so many outstanding players. . . . Ted Williams stood ceiling-high. He very rarely looked back at an umpire at the plate. And he would help you even to the point of getting players off your back. If you finished the season with Boston, he'd come to the dressing room, shake your hand, wish you and your family a happy winter, and thank you for being associated with the game. He was the only one to ever do that."

Had Ted not missed the 1943, 1944 and 1945 seasons while serving in the Navy during World War II, he almost certainly would have had another 100 home runs—to which he might have added yet another 50 had he not spent most of 1952 and 1953 serving in the Korean War. Ted actually did hit one home run at Fenway Park during a 1943 game, but you won't find it in any record books. To support the war effort, the Boston Braves played a special team of all-stars drawn from the armed services. Ted played on the all-star team and hit a home run. His manager? Babe Ruth.

In his book *Cobb*, A.L. Stump asserts that Ted and Ty Cobb had a bitter falling out over an incident in which they were comparing their all-time line-ups. Williams argued for the inclusion of Rogers Hornsby on his all-star squad. Cobb objected, presumably due to his intense personal dislike for Hornsby. Ted, probably unaware of this and arguing his point, added recklessly that Hornsby's .424 season had even outdone the Georgia Peach. Cobb, the story goes, became enraged, shouting "Get away from me! And don't come back!" And he never spoke to Ted again. Ted refutes this version, telling Jim Prime, "Ty Cobb was a close friend of mine and we remained friends up until the time he died."

When Ted tried his hand on the pitching mound in an August game in 1940, his catcher was Joe Glenn, the same man who had caught the final pitch thrown by another pretty good hitter named Babe Ruth. Glenn was a catcher for the Yankees in 1933, the last year Ruth appeared on the mound in a major league game.

In 1954 Ted Williams reported to spring training and on the first day of workouts, fell in the outfield and broke his collarbone. He was sent back to Boston where doctors inserted a steel pin in his shoulder, and as a result Williams missed all of spring training. After a period of recuperation, he took batting practice for a few days and rejoined the Red Sox in Baltimore, where he was put in to pinch-hit. He flied out to center field.

The Red Sox then moved on to Detroit for a double header against the Tigers. It was during this twin bill that the Red Sox leftfielder single-handedly set spring training back 50 years. Ted went 8 for 9 in what announcer Curt Gowdy calls, "The most amazing batting show I think I've ever seen.

"Before the game," recalls Gowdy, "I asked him how he felt and he was moaning. 'Oh, I'm not swinging the bat well. I shouldn't even be playing.' And then he goes out and hits every pitch they throw to him. The New York Yankees were playing the Indians in Cleveland, and the next morning Casey Stengel was reading about Ted's feat in the morning paper. The old perfessor said, 'I'm gonna get them steel pins put in all my players' shoulders.'"

Even superstars took a backseat to Ted Williams. American League MVP Jackie Jensen once confided to roommate Dick Gernert: "You crouch in the on-deck circle and watch them throw four wide pitches past the big guy, and you think of your kid days, when the other pitchers were afraid of you. With Williams on your side, they're never afraid of you up there. They'd rather pitch to anyone but him. Then if you don't get on base yourself, you're the goat." —from *The Jackie Jensen Story*

Ted was famous for his great eye at the plate. He seldom swung at any pitch that wasn't in the strike zone and pitchers knew this all too well. So did umpires, who respected his patience and his infallible knowledge of the strike zone. The Yankees were about to play the Red Sox and during a clubhouse meeting they were going over the various hitters. Catcher Bill Dickey advised pitcher Spud Chandler to pitch Ted either "high and tight" or "low and away. " Chandler, one of the Yankees' best hurlers, was not impressed with this advice. "Ok, Bill," he said sarcastically. "I throw one high and tight, and the next one low and away. Now it's two balls and no strikes. Then what do I do?"

Hall of Famer Jim Palmer recalls: "The first time I met Ted was when he was managing the Washington Senators. He was giving a hitting clinic and I remember telling him our second baseman, Davey Johnson, that you need to have a six-degree upswing. Davey worked hard on that. He had about 148 different batting stances for the year trying to get that six-degree upswing. He'd swing and then he'd ask me, 'You think that's six degrees?' and I'd say, 'No. It's only about five and a half.'"

Even the best hitter in history had his off days. The only player in ML history to face a pitcher three times in the same inning? Ted Williams. He set the major league record in the seventh inning of an Independence Day game between Boston and Washington. Ted walked twice and grounded out once. The Red Sox scored 14 times that inning, but Ted didn't have a hit in the entire game—the only Red Sox player who didn't.

"I am building up strength to do a lot of slamming as we head down the stretch," Ted said in late July 1946. "Thursday night down at Pawtucket," Mel Webb wrote in the *Boston Globe,* "he did as well in the banquet league as he has been doing all along at the dish. And here's the damage Teddy did:

3 shrimp cocktails
3 cups of fish chowder

1   1 1/2 inch thick steak
10 rolls
1 pound of butter
2 orders of string beans
2   2 1/2 pound broiled lobsters
1 chef's salad
3 ice creams with chocolate sauce
plus an undetermined amount of iced tea

Legendary Sox announcer and longtime friend of Ted Williams, Curt Gowdy recalls a phone call he received a few years ago from the erstwhile "Kid." "Seven a.m.," he says. "I was sound asleep. I heard this gruff voice, 'Gowdy! It's Teddy Ballgame. Wake up! I want to ask you something. Where in the hell are those golden years?' And then he hung up."

Rick Wise

Rick Wise was a talented right-handed pitcher who won 188 games during his 18-year major league career. From 1974-77, he pitched for the Red Sox, winning 19 games for the pennant winners of 1975.

While with the Red Sox, Wise was a member of the infamous group known as the "Buffalo Heads" who succeeded in making manager Don Zimmer's life less than pleasant during his time in Boston. Other members were Bill Lee and Ferguson Jenkins. The group was supposedly named after Zimmer because, as Jenkins so kindly put it, "a buffalo is the dumbest animal on earth."

Perhaps Wise should have thought back to his own baseball past before joining such a group. While pitching in the National League against San Francisco he was once hit in the head by a line drive and was immediately rushed to the hospital where x-rays were taken. Fortunately the results were negative, but when Wise opened the newspaper the next day, he was confronted with the following sports page headline: "X-rays of Wise's Head Reveal Nothing."

Smoky Joe Wood

"Smoky Joe could throw harder than anyone."— Satchel Paige

"I threw so hard I thought my arm would fly right off my body."—Joe Wood

Wood shared one thing with Babe Ruth—they were both excellent pitchers *and* excellent hitters. Ruth is more known for his hitting career, obviously, but—largely in his years with Boston—he did win 94 games to just 46 losses and posted a 2.28 career ERA! Smoky Joe Wood, on the other hand, is remembered only as a pitcher; he had precisely the same win-percentage ratio as Ruth (.671) with a 116-57 record and a career 2.03 ERA. He's best remembered for his spectacular 34-5 season for the Red Sox in 1912, with 344 innings pitched. Nevertheless, Wood was also a good hitter. Back in those days, the pitcher always hit

Smoky Joe Wood (Brace Photography)

anyhow, but after the Red Sox sold his contract to Cleveland before the 1917 season, Wood played the outfield and hit a respectable .297 over six seasons. His lifetime average was .283.

Smoky Joe Wood and Babe Ruth both appeared for the Red Sox in one World Series as pitchers and in another World Series as outfielders.

Tris and Smoky

Surely the most productive roommates in Red Sox history were Tris Speaker and Smoky Joe Wood. In 1912, the two friends led the Red Sox to the American League pennant and a World Series championship. Wood won 34 regular-season games and notched three World Series victories. He pitched 35 complete games during the season, and boasted a microscopic 1.91 ERA. Speaker batted .383 and, in the middle of the dead ball era, led the A.L. in doubles with 53, and homers with 10.

Joseph Frank Wood, the son of Red Sox fireballer Smoky Joe Wood, pitched three games for the Red Sox in 1944. This Wood was hardly a chip off the old block. He went 0-1 with a 6.52 ERA.

John Wyatt

Caught in a rundown between third and home, pitcher John Wyatt dropped several items from his Sox pitching jacket. The excess baggage included a tube of Vaseline, a pack of cigarettes and his car keys. We're not sure what Sherlock Holmes would deduce from those clues, but possibly, just possibly, Wyatt was up to no good.

Carl Yastrzemski

"He arrived in Boston to fill a void. He departed leaving one."—Friend & Zminda

Newspapers regularly misspelled his name, but in box scores he was usually Y'str'mski. When Carl Yastrzemski retired at the end of the 1983 baseball season, people throughout baseball paid tribute to his 23-year career. Perhaps it was Tony La Russa, then White Sox manager and one of the most astute baseball minds of our time, who paid him the most fitting compliment. "I have a little quirk when filling out my lineup cards for the opposing team. I never use vowels except for Yastrzemski. I just feel it would be disrespectful to him not to spell his name out. As a Red Sox fan back in 1967, I remember vividly every hit he got that year. All through his career he's been a game-breaker."

On the eve of his retirement, Yaz recalled some of his best catches and most important hits for the *Boston Herald*.

Defensive Plays:
#1 "The best was the play I made off Reggie Jackson in the third game of the '75 playoffs. " This was the game in

which he cut off a ball that looked like a sure two-run triple and held Jackson to a single. After the game, Jackson allowed that "only two people could have made that play: Carl Yastrzemski and God."

#2 " The diving catch in Yankee Stadium off Tom Tresh in the opening game of the 1967 "Impossible Dream" season." The catch temporarily preserved a no-hitter by Red Sox rookie pitcher Billy Rohr. Rohr lost the no-hitter on a hit by Elston Howard with two out in the ninth inning, but many people point to this game and this play as the inspiration for the rest of this miracle "cardiac kids" campaign.

Biggest Hits:
"Just about every hit I had in 1967 could be the biggest," Yaz rightly says. "But I'd say the top five were the three-run homer off Jim Merritt on the second-to-last day of the 1967 season; the bases-loaded single which tied the game the next day; the two-out, ninth-inning homer off Fred Lasher that tied a game in Detroit earlier that year (Dalton Jones won it with a homer in the 11th); my home run off Vida Blue in the 1975 playoffs when we were losing 3-0; and my 400th homer off Oakland's Mike Morgan not only because it was the 400th but because it won a game in a pennant race." *Boston Herald* Oct. 2, 1983

Now playing third base: Carl Yastrzemski. When Rico was hurt in 1973, Yaz filled in for 11 games. He logged ten errors.

Carl owned a car dealership in Massachusetts named Yaz Ford. Every time the team would be on the bus and pass an auto junkyard, Luis Tiant would shout out, "Hey, there's Yaz Ford. Nah, that can't be it. Those cars look better than the ones you've got."

In *Tales From the Red Sox Dugout*, we told about an incident involving Yaz and slicing up clothing, which related to Doug Griffin. Another time after several players had sliced up each others' clothes, Yaz walked through the hotel lobby with his shirt and sweater all torn. Luis Aparicio was with him. By coincidence, the Miss Minnesota pageant had just spilled out and a few of the losing contestants were in the lobby sobbing. Gary Peters said hello to them, then added, "Don't feel bad. Look at these guys. I just dragged them off the street to have a meal."

Another time in Minneapolis, Yaz had cut up all of Peters' clothing and stuffed them in his suitcase. Out for dinner the next night, Peters (who'd never said a word about it) excused himself, grabbed a cab and shot over to the team's hotel. He cut up Yaz's clothes, and then set fire to them in the middle of the room but found himself unable to extinguish the flames. Just then Yaz, who'd followed his instinct, burst into the room and found the mess.

The next morning, Yaz checked out very early. When he got to the park, the police and a fire chief were waiting. Yaz said the mess was due to a can of Sterno they'd knocked over warming some fish.

"Carl Yastrzemski is the only guy in baseball who can not only read an eye chart but understand it. He's retiring from baseball because they won't let him grow potatoes in left field. Anyone who spends 20 years running into a wall has to be lonely."—Don Rickles

Carl is the last player in baseball to win the coveted Triple Crown. He accomplished the feat in 1967, hitting 44 homers (tied for first with Minnesota's Harmon Killebrew), 121 RBIs and a .326 batting average.

The 1968 season was a pitcher's dream and a hitter's nightmare. Carl Yastrzemski batted .301 and led the American League in batting! No other player, not even a part-timer reached the .300 standard that season. Yaz's teammate Ken Harrelson led the circuit in RBIs with a modest total of 109 and actually finished seventh in the batting race with a .275 average!

Yaz, sadly, made the final out in the 1967 World Series, the 1975 World Series and the 1978 one-day playoff against the Yankees to determine the pennant winner.

In 1978 Buddy LeRoux, then vice-president and part owner of the Red Sox was telling a Polish joke in the locker room at Fenway Park. LeRoux is speaking loud enough to ensure that the most famous Pole in the room hears every word. When the joke it completed, Carl Yastrzemski turns to his tormentor and says "I got something for you, Buddy. I'll leave it in your office. I'm on the way there now." With that Yastrzemski gets up from his chair and walks past LeRoux into the washroom.—*Sport*, October 1978

Carl Yastrzemski (Brace Photography)

The two best-remembered exits by Red Sox stars couldn't have been more different. In 1960, Ted Williams hit a home run in this last at-bat and refused to tip his hat to adoring fans. When Yaz left in 1983, he did it with less fanfare but more *savoir faire,* circling the field and shaking hands with fans.

Yaz Jazz:

"YAZ, SIR, THAT'S MY BABY." —sign seen at Fenway during '67 season.

"Ed (Runge), you're the second best umpire in the league. The other 23 are tied for first."

"I knew when the ball was going out [over the Green Monster]. It was something I worked into the decoy, but it used to tick the pitchers off.

"Bill Monbouquette used to say, 'Can't you at least make it look like you can catch it?' Meanwhile, the ball would be on its way over the fence to a spot three-quarters of the way out to the railroad tracks."

"I'm very pleased and very proud of my accomplishments, but I'm most proud of that [hitting 400 home runs and 3,000 hits]. Not [Ted] Williams, not [Lou] Gehrig, not [Joe] DiMaggio did that. They were Cadillacs and I'm a Chevrolet."

"I think about baseball when I wake up in the morning. I think about it all day and I dream about it at night. The only time I don't think about it is when I'm playing it."

"The 3,000 hit thing was the first time I let individual pressure get to me. I was uptight about it. When I saw the hit going through, I had a sigh of relief more than anything."

"They can talk about Babe Ruth and Ty Cobb and Rogers Hornsby and Lou Gehrig and Joe DiMaggio and

Stan Musial and all the rest, but I'm sure not one of them could hold cards and spades to Williams in his sheer knowledge of hitting. He studied hitting the way a broker studies the stock market, and could spot at a glance mistakes that others couldn't see in a week."

"And if I have my choice between a pennant and a triple crown, I'll take the pennant every time."

Tom Yawkey

When Tom Yawkey ran the ball club, it was a different era, with the reserve rule in place and no sports agents mediating between the players and the ball club. Yawkey was very wealthy, though he remained a down-to-earth guy who didn't put on airs and could readily be mistaken for one of the clubhouse attendants. He was also very generous with players and as a result, a strong loyalty was returned. At the end of Johnny Pesky's first year with the Red Sox, he was changing in the clubhouse and was sent a message to come upstairs. Ballplayers weren't allowed upstairs without being summoned, so Johnny was understandably apprehensive. Eddie Collins gave him an envelope from Mr. Yawkey. Inside, the rookie found a bonus check, enough to buy his parents a house to live in back in Portland, Oregon.

Even Sparky Anderson, after his Cincinnati Reds had just defeated the Boston Red Sox in the 1975 World Series paused to praise Yawkey. "Tom Yawkey was the greatest gentleman I've ever met in baseball," said Sparky.

Tom Yawkey (Brace Photography)

Tom Yawkey was owner of the Boston Red Sox but he was also a baseball fan who loved to hang out with ballplayers. This created numerous problems for manager Joe Cronin, according to Cronin's daughter Maureen:

"Tom Yawkey was a bit of a rascal so it was tough on dad. He'd be trying to get the players to come in at a certain time and the players would be out drinking with Tom Yawkey. A couple of times it was funny because dad would be waiting up in the hotel lobby and in would come Tom with a player and dad couldn't really say much about that. Guys like Mickey McDermott and Walt Dropo would probably admit that they drove dad a bit crazy. Yawkey loved the ballplayers. He used to like to go down into the clubhouse and wrestle with them."

Rudy York

Rudy York once drove in an astounding 10 runs in a single 1946 game against the St. Louis Browns. But the amazing part is that he had done that by the fifth inning and still had two more plate appearances coming. York started his incredible day with a grand slam in the second inning. He followed that with another grand salami in the fifth frame. Both round-trippers came at the expense of Browns reliever Tex Shirley. Rudy struck out in the seventh with one man on, and hit into a double play with two on in the ninth.

Of the 11 major league players who have hit two grand slams in a single game, two others were Red Sox: Jim Tabor in 1939 and Nomar Garciaparra in 1999.

Cy Young

Born just a few years after the end of the Civil War, the 6-2, 210-pound Cy Young pitched in the major leagues for 22 years with five different clubs and averaged more than eight innings a game during that stretch! Young once pitched a record 24 consecutive innings without yielding a hit.

On June 13, 1903 when his 361st career win eclipsed Pud Galvin's 360th, Cy Young became the pitcher with the most wins in baseball history; nearly 100 years later, no one has challenged him for that distinction. Meanwhile, Cobb's record for the most career hits, Ruth's for the most home runs, even Lou Gehrig's for the most consecutive games played—all of these cumulative triumphs have all been surpassed.

Young also holds the distinction of having pitched the first inning of the first official World Series game, in 1903. What could be more appropriate than having the man whose name is synonymous with pitching throw the very first pitch ever thrown in World Series competition? Although he gave up an uncharacteristic four runs, he did win two games and lose one in the 1903 Series. He held a 1.85 ERA in 34 postseason innings that year.

In 1904, the Red Sox pitching staff threw a phenomenal 148 complete games (this was when there were only 154 games each year.) The entire *team* had an earned run average of 2.12 and only surrendered 233 walks in 1406 innings of play. The Sox posted 21 shutouts. Forty one— yes, 41—of the complete games were authored by Cy Young! Young's biographer Reed Browning states that he retired 76 consecutive hitters without a hit over 24 innings as part of a stretch in which he threw 45 consecutive scoreless innings. This is the *equivalent of five consecutive complete game shutouts!* For good measure he also tossed a perfect game during this stretch.

Obviously, the man whose name now symbolizes excellence in the art of pitching was a great pitcher himself. In June of 1908 at the ripe old baseball age of 41, Young threw his third no-hitter, this one against the New York Highlanders in New York. Young began the game by walking the first batter, Harry Niles. Niles was quickly erased trying to steal second base. Young then confounded the remainder of the Highlanders' line-up en route to an 8-0 gem.

Cy Young's 511 wins—his 192 wins for Boston puts him in a direct tie with Roger Clemens for top spot in that category—is such a staggering total that a pitcher would have to be a 20-game winner for 25 straight years and then win another 12 games the year after that to top him. Pitchers can have long careers—Nolan Ryan pitched for 27 years, but he "only" won 324 games. Young threw 749 complete games; Ryan only appeared in 807 total (but an impressive 222 of those were complete games.)

In fact, Young pitched in so many games that he also holds the records for the most losses of any pitcher: 315. Not surprisingly, Ryan is close behind with 292. Nevertheless, Cy's .619 winning percentage was outstanding by anyone's standards.

Young hinted that he was not above using any method available to get batters out. "I admit that some of my cutplug tobacco would get on the ball."

In 1908, a "Cy Young Day" was held for Young at the old Huntington Avenue Grounds in Boston. Over 20,000 fans turned out to honor the man who had gone 22-15 the previous season, and had finished with a 21-11 record in '08—with a no-hitter thrown in. Not bad for a 41-year-old man! In fact the old Young was almost as good as the young Young: at age 41, in 1908, he pitched 30 complete games and posted a yearlong ERA of just 1.26. *Sporting Life*, poking fun at Young's longevity, commented after his 1911 season, "The old boy is said to look better than any previous season since 1663, considered by many to be his best year since the Summer of 1169." Young received various gifts on that day, including about $7,500 in cash. The most telling gift however was presented by the American League umpires association—a traveling bag. Cy was sold that fall to Cleveland for $12,500.

Don Zimmer

Bill Lee and Don Zimmer were like oil and water; they just didn't mix. Zimmer is the prototypical old school manager who respects the unwritten rules and traditions of the game; Lee was as close as baseball gets to a wild-eyed radical. Lee once labeled Zimmer "the gerbil" and was generally a very large thorn in his side throughout his tenure in Beantown.

In Zimmer's recent book *Zim*, the former Red Sox manager and current Yankee bench coach exacts a measure of verbal revenge on his tormentor, referring to Lee as the "only man I've ever known in baseball who I wouldn't let in my house." Asked if he'd read the book, Lee replied: "No, I didn't. I don't read fiction." He had heard about it, though, and offered the following review. "I've sold a hundred thousand copies of that book for him just by that one line. Hey, I love it. You've gotta check the source. He had a lot of Richard Nixon in him. Hell, to be praised by a Yankee is damnable." He added: "Zimmer wouldn't know a good pitcher if he came up and bit him in the ass."

Is there any chance of reconciliation between the Spaceman and Zim? According to Lee, the answer is no. "I've tried. The veins in his neck just get real big. I can see him on life support and some Red Sox fan runs in and says, 'The Spaceman is here to see you.' Instant straight line!"

At the beginning of the 1977 season, Zimmer had to make the agonizing decision to release longtime Red Sox third baseman Rico Petrocelli in favor of young and offensively more potent Butch Hobson. The decision was not well received throughout New England and Zimmer received death threats. One was very specific, claiming that Zimmer would be shot while getting off the plane in Boston after spring training. When the plane arrived, Zimmer confronted Jim Rice, the Boston strongman and one of Zimmer's favorites, asking him to get off the plane in front of him. "My ass!" replied Rice. "I'm not taking no bullet for you!"

Bill Zuber/Bob Zupcic

When he joined the big league club at the very end of the 1991 campaign, Bob Zupcic erased a distinction pitcher Bill Zuber had held for nearly 50 years: since 1947 Zuber had always been the final entry in any comprehensive listing of Red Sox players. "Goober" Zuber came over from the Yankees in time to go 5-1 on the 1946 pennant-winning Red Sox team. He was born and raised in Middle Amana, Iowa, one of the few communal societies in the United States. Zuber's, a restaurant he founded, still flourishes in the area. Zupcic tied a major league mark for freshmen ballplayers in 1992, his official rookie season, when he hit two grand slams.

Sox Populi

"The hardest thing to do in baseball is to hit a round baseball with a round bat, squarely."

—Ted Williams

"I gave $250 to some mission in Alaska. I wouldn't send the fine to Bowie Kuhn because it might end up in a Nixon re-election campaign."   —Bill Lee

"When I was young, I'd spend summer weekends shagging flies and pretending I was Carl Yastrzemski. Now I spend them mowing the lawn and pretending I'm Joe Mooney.   —Dan Seidman

"Pope dead, Sox Alive, details at 11."

—Charles Laquidara, WBCN announcer, after the slumping Red Sox rallied to beat Toronto in a crucial series during their ill-fated drive for the 1978 pennant.

"When he (Nomar) called to say he was coming to Georgia Tech, I turned to my wife, Gina, and said, 'Nobody knows this yet, but we just got our best player ever.'"

—Rick Jones, former Georgia Tech Baseball Coach

"We are the best team in baseball."

—Cincinnati Reds manager Sparky Anderson on the eve of the 1975 World Series.

"We are the best team in baseball. But not by much."

—Sparky Anderson after his team captured the 1975 World Series in seven hard-fought games.

"After my career, I didn't walk down streets. I walked down alleys."

—Bob Uecker, when asked if he shared Ted Williams' dream of walking down the street after his career was over and having people say, "There goes the greatest hitter who ever lived."

"Defensively, the Red Sox are a lot like Stonehenge. They are old, they don't move, and no one is certain why they are positioned the way they are.

—*Boston Globe* writer Dan Shaughnessy describes an unlamented Red Sox team of the of the early nineties

"If I could play shortstop like him (Nomar Garciaparra), that's what I would like to do."

—Pedro Martinez

"Yaz, you're my idol. I want my son to be just like you — rich!"

—Red Sox outfielder Joe Foy,
to all-star Carl Yastrzemski

"The Red Sox stranded more men than Zsa Zsa Gabor."

—Yankee owner George Steinbrenner on the Red Sox performance in Game Six of the 1986 World Series.

"They killed our fathers and now the sons of bitches are coming after us."

—a New Haven bar owner reflecting the trauma and paranoia inherent in being a Red Sox fan. (as quoted by Peter Gammons after the '78 playoff with the Yankees.)

"Baseball is the only field of endeavor where a man can succeed three times out of ten and be considered a good performer."

—Ted Williams

"*Fear Strikes Out* is the worst movie ever made about baseball."

—Jimmy Piersall

Just the Facts

The Red Sox scored 23 runs in a single postseason game in '99. According to *Baseball America*, there have been nine postseason series in which the two teams combined failed to score 23 runs in the entire series.

The following Red Sox players have had their numbers retired: Joe Cronin (#4) 1935-1945, Ted Williams (#9) 1939-1960, Bobby Doerr (#1) 1937-1951, Carl Yastrzemski (#8) 1961-1983. Carlton Fisk (#27) 1969-1980 with the Red Sox.

"As long as I'm playing ball, it doesn't matter where I am, as long as it's not in a Yankees uniform."

—Carl Everett

"Whenever I feel my ego getting away with me, I call my mom and ask if I can take out the trash."

—Nomar Garciaparra

"I like it when the pitcher thinks he has given up a hit and, the next thing you know, I'm throwing the guy out. The pitcher gets so excited. You can see it in his face."

— Nomar Garciaparra

"I'm just tired of seeing New York always win."

—Manny Ramirez

Jokes

There was a Texan, a New Yorker and a Bostonian in a sports bar drinking. The Texan throws back a shot of tequila, throws the half full bottle up in the air, takes out a gun and shoots the bottle to bits. The New Yorker and the Bostonian look at him in amazement when he says, "Where I come from we have plenty of tequila."

Not to be outdone, the New Yorker took off his Yankees cap, tossed back the rest of his glass of Merlot, then tosses the half full bottle of wine in the air, takes out his gun and blows it to bits. He says, "Where I come from we have plenty of fine wine."

The Bostonian slowly finishes his beer, tugs his Sox cap down snugly, takes the rest of the six pack, throws it in the air, takes out his gun and shoots the New Yorker between the eyes, then catches the six pack. He turns to the stunned Texan and says, "Where I come from we don't waste good beer, but we have too many Yankees fans."

Three baseball fans were on their way to a game when one noticed a foot sticking out of the bushes by the side of the road. They stopped and discovered a nude female dead. Out of respect and propriety, the Cubs fan took off his cap and placed it over her right breast. The Red Sox fan took off his cap and placed it over her left breast. Following their lead, the Yankees fan took off his cap and placed it over her crotch.

The police were called and when the officer arrived, he conducted his inspection. First, he lifted up the Cubs cap, replaced it, and wrote down some notes. Next, he lifted the Sox cap, replaced it, and wrote down some more notes.

The officer then lifted the Yankees cap, replaced it, then lifted it again, replaced it, lifted it a third time, and replaced it one last time. The Yankee fan was getting upset and finally asked, "What are you, a pervert or something? Why do you keep lifting and looking, lifting and looking?" "Well," said the officer, "I am simply surprised. Normally when I look under a Yankees hat, I find an a—hole."

A first-grade teacher in New York City explains to her class that she and her husband are excited about the year 2000 World Series because she is a Mets fan and her husband is a Yankees fan. She asks her students to raise their hands if they, too, are either Mets or Yankees fans.

Everyone in the class raises their hands except one little girl. The teacher looks at the girl with surprise and asks, "Janie, why didn't you raise your hand?"

"Because I'm not a Mets or Yankees fan," she replies.

The teacher, still shocked, asks, "Well, if you are not a Mets or Yankees fan, then who are you a fan of?"

"I am a Red Sox fan, and proud of it," Janie replied.

The teacher cannot believe her ears. "Janie, why are you a Red Sox fan?"

"Because my mom is a Red Sox fan, and my dad is a Red Sox fan, so I'm a Red Sox fan, too!"

"Well," says the teacher in an obviously annoyed tone, "that is no reason for you to be a Red Sox fan. You don't have to be just like your parents all of the time. What if your mom were a moron and your dad were a moron — what would you be then?"

"Then," Janie smiled, 'We'd be Mets and Yankees fans."

Two young boys are playing baseball on a vacant lot in a Boston suburb. Suddenly one of the boys is attacked by a rabid Rottweiler. As the vicious dog is about to finish off his helpless victim, the other boy takes his bat, wedges it into the dog's collar and gives it a mighty twist, breaking the dog's neck.

A reporter who witnessed the dramatic event dashes across the street to interview the young hero. He starts writing in his notepad: "Young Red Sox Fan Saves Friend From Vicious Animal".

Looking over the reporter's shoulder, the young boy protested: "But I'm not a Red Sox fan." "Sorry," replies the reporter. "I assumed that everyone in Boston was a Red Sox fan." "Not me," replied the boy proudly, "I cheer for the world champion New York Yankees!"

Without hesitation, the resourceful reporter crossed out the headline and wrote: "Little New York Bastard Kills Beloved Family Pet".

A man from Boston dies and goes to Hell. The devil ushers him into a room and says: "I hope you're prepared for some pretty hot temperatures." The man replies: "No problem, I'm from Boston."

The devil leaves the room and turns the thermostat up to 100 and the humidity to 80. He returns 15 minutes later and asks the Bostonian how he's doing.

"No problem. Boston gets this warm in June." A bit surprised, the devil goes out and turns the thermostat up to 150 and the humidity to 90. Again the devil asks the man from Boston how he's doing. "Just like Beantown in July," the man replies. "Makes me feel right at home." Frustrated, the devil cranks the heat up to 200 degrees and the humidity to 100. When he looks in the room, he sees that the guy from Boston has removed his shirt and there is some sweat on his brow, but he still seems to be enjoying the weather. "Just like Boston in August," he says dreamily. By now the devil is at the end of his rope. He goes back to the thermostat and turns it to minus 150 degrees. All of Hell immediately freezes solid, and even the devil himself is shivering. To his complete amazement, he opens the door and sees the Bostonian jumping up and down in ecstasy. "What could you possibly be so happy about?" demands the devil. The man replies: "THE RED SOX WON THE WORLD SERIES! THE RED SOX WON THE WORLD SERIES!"

One day four baseball fans were climbing a mountain. Each was a fan of a different team in the A.L. East and each proclaimed to be the most loyal of all fans of their baseball team.

As they climbed higher, they argued as to which one of them was the most loyal of all. They continued to argue all the way up the mountain, and finally as they reached the top, the Toronto fan hurled himself off the mountain, shouting, "This is for the Jays!" as he fell to his doom. Not wanting to be outdone, the Baltimore fan threw himself off the mountain, proclaiming, "This is for the O's!"

Seeing this, the Boston fan walked over and shouted, "This is for THE SOX!" . . . and pushed the Yankee fan off the side of the mountain.

The Boston Symphony Orchestra was performing Beethoven's Ninth. In the piece, there's a passage about 20 minutes long during which the bass violinists have nothing to do. Rather than sit around the whole time looking stupid, some bassists decided to sneak offstage and go to the tavern next door, grab a quick beer and catch an inning of the Sox on TV. After slamming several ales in quick succession, one of them looked at his watch. "Hey! We need to get back!"

"No need to panic," said his fellow bassist, "I thought we might need some extra time, so I tied the last few pages of Seiji's score together (Sox fan Seiji Ozawa) with string. It'll take him a few minutes to get it untangled." A few minutes later they staggered back to the concert hall and took their places in the orchestra. About the same time, a member of the audience noticed the conductor seemed a bit edgy, fussing with things, and said as much to her companion. "Well of course," said her companion. "Don't you see? It's the bottom of the Ninth, the score is tied, and the bassists are loaded! "

Bibliography

The following newspapers and magazines were consulted frequently: *Boston Globe, Boston Herald, Boston Post, Diehard, Sport, The Sporting News,* and *Sports Illustrated,* for which we also thank the Boston Public Library and the Tufts University Library.

These books served as sources:

Anderson, Sparky. *Sparky!* (NY: Prentice-Hall, 1990)

Auker, Elden with Tom Keegan. *Sleeper Cars and Flannel Uniforms* (Chicago: Triumph Books, 2001)

Berry, Henry. *Boston Red Sox* (NY: Collier Books, 1975)

Broeg, Bob. *Superstars of Baseball* (St. Louis:The Sporting News, 1971)

Browning, Reed. *Cy Young* (Amherst: University of Massachusetts Press, 2000)

Caren, Eric C. *Baseball Extra* (Edison, NJ: Castle Books, 2000)

Chadwick, Bruce & David M. Spindel. *The Boston Red Sox* (NY: Abbeville Press, 1992)

Chapman, Con. *The Year of the Gerbil* (Danbury CT: Rutledge Books, 1998)

Clemens, Roger with Peter Gammons. *Rocket Man* (VT: The Stephen Greene Press, 1987)

Connor, Floyd. *Baseball's Most Wanted* (Washington D.C.: Brassey's, 2000)

Corbett, Bernard M. *Red Sox Trivia* (Boston: Quinlan, 1986)

Friend, Luke and Don Zminda. *The Best Book of Baseball Facts & Stats* (Carlton Books, 2000)

Gallen, David (Ed.). *The Baseball Chronicles* (NY: Carroll & Graf, 1991)

Gerlach, Larry R. *The Men in Blue* (Lincoln & London: University of Nebraska Press, 1994)

Grossman, Leigh. *The Red Sox Fan Handbook* (Pomfret, CT: Swordsmith, 2001)

Harrelson, Ken and Al Hirshberg. *Hawk* (NY: Viking, 1969)

Hirshberg, Al. *The Jackie Jensen Story* (NY: Julian Messner, 1960)

Holway, John R. *The Baseball Astrologer* (Kingston NY: Total Sports Illustrated, 2000)

Horvitz, Peter S. and Joachim Horvitz. *The Big Book of Jewish Baseball* (NY; SPI Books, 2001)

Lyons, Steve. *Psycho-analysis* (Champaign, IL: Sagamore Publishing, 1995)

Martin, George I. *The Golden Boy* (Portsmouth NH: Peter E. Randall Publisher, 2000)

McCullough, Bob. *My Greatest Day in Baseball* (Dallas: Taylor Publishing, 1998)

Moffi, Larry. *This Side of Cooperstown* (Ames, Iowa: University of Iowa Press, 1996)

Nelson, Kevin. *Baseball's Greatest Insults* (NY: Fireside Books, 1984)

Okrent, Daniel & Steve Wulf. *Baseball Anecdotes* (NY & Oxford: Oxford University Press, 1989)

Peary, Danny (Ed.). *They Played the Game* (NY: Hyperion, 1994)

Phelan, Rick. *A Bittersweet Journey* (Tampa: McGregor: 2000)

Prime, Jim & Bill Nowlin. *Ted Williams: A Tribute* (Indianapolis: Masters Press, 1997)

Prime, Jim and Ted Williams. *Ted Williams' Hit List* (Indianapolis: Masters Press, 1996)

Rucker, Mark and Peter Bjarkman. *Smoke* (NY: Total Sports Illustrated, 1999)

Sampson, Arthur. *Ted Williams* (NY: A. S. Barnes, 1950)

Shalin, Bruce. *Oddballs* (NY: Penguin Books, 1989)

Smith, Curt. *Our House* (Chicago: Masters Press, 1999)

Solomon, Burt. *The Baseball Timeline* (London, NY, etc.: DK Publishing, 2001)

Stout, Glenn & Richard Johnson. *Red Sox Century* (Boston: Houghton Mifflin, 2001)

Sullivan, George. *The Picture History of the Boston Red Sox* (NY: Bobbs-Merrill, 1980)

Tiant, Luis and Joe Fitzgerald. *El Tiante* (NY: Doubleday, 1976)

Walton, Ed. *Red Sox Triumphs and Tragedies* (NY: Scarborough, 1980)

Walton, Ed. *This Date in Red Sox History* (NY: Scarborough, 1978)

Werber, Bill and C. Paul Rogers III. *Memories Of A Ballplayer* (Cleveland: Society for American Baseball Research, 2001)

Williams, Dick and Bill Plaschke. *No More Mr. Nice Guy* (San Diego, NY and London: Harcourt Brace Jovanovich, 1990)

Williams, Ted with John Underwood. *My Turn At Bat* (NY: Fireside, 1988)

Yastrzemski, Carl and Gerald Eskenazi. *Yaz: Baseball, The Wall and Me* (NY: Doubleday, 1990)

Zimmer, Don with Bill Madden. *Zim* (Kingston NY: Total Sports Publishing, 2001)

Zingg, Paul J. *Harry Hooper* (Urbana: University of Illinois Press, 1995)

Our definitive statistical source was *Total Baseball*, seventh edition, edited by John Thorn, Pete Palmer and Michael Gershman with Matthew Silverman, Sean Lahman and Greg Spira (Kingston NY: Total Sports Publishing, 2001)

We consulted the following websites for information of one kind or another: www.baseballalmanac.com; www.baseball-reference.com ; www.redsox.com; www.redsoxdiehard.com; www.redsoxgripe.com; www.whereisroger.com; www.sports.espn.go.com

Celebrate the Heroes of Baseball
in These Other Acclaimed Titles from Sports Publishing!